ANNMARIE ADAMS and PETA TANCRED

'Designing Women'

Gender and the
Architectural Profession

UNIVERSITY OF TORONTO PRESS
Toronto Buffalo London

© University of Toronto Press Incorporated 2000
Toronto Buffalo London

Printed in Canada

ISBN 0-8020-4417-4 (cloth)
ISBN 0-8020-8219-X (paper)

Printed on acid-free paper

Canadian Cataloguing in Publication Data

Adams, Annmarie
    Designing women : gender and the architectural profession

    Includes bibliographical references and index.
    ISBN 0-8020-4417-4 (bound)   ISBN 0-8020-8219-X (pbk.)

    1. Women architects – Canada. I. Tancred, Peta, 1937–   . II. Title.

    NA1997.A32 2000   720′.82   C99-932936-7

Chapter 3 appeared previously as 'Building Barriers: Images of Women in the *RAIC Journal*, 1924–73' in *Resources for Feminist Research* 23/2 (Fall, 1994), and as 'Les Representations des femmes dans la revue de l'Institute Royal Architectural du Canada, 1924–73,' in *Recherche féministes* 7/2 (1994). Usage by permission.

The University of Toronto Press acknowledges the financial assistance to its publishing program of the Canada Council for the Arts and the Ontario Arts Council.

This book has been published with the help of a grant from the Humanities and Social Sciences Federation of Canada, using funds provided by the Social Sciences and Humanities Research Council of Canada.

University of Toronto Press acknowledges the financial support for its publishing activities of the Government of Canada through the Book Publishing Industry Development Program (BPIDP).

To our mothers,
Kaye Adams and the late Elma Tancred,
innovators before their time

Contents

List of Tables

Acknowledgments

This book, and the research on which it is based, would not have been possible without the cooperation of many individuals and institutions. First, we would like to acknowledge the McGill Centre for Research and Teaching on Women, which proved to be an inspiring and supportive base for this project over many years. We are particularly indebted to Nora Brown, Monica Hotter, Abby Lippman, Shree Mulay, and Blossom Shaffer for their support of this study. Feminist, interdisciplinary projects such as ours would be much more difficult, if not impossible, undertakings without the centre's positive presence as a forum for women's issues at McGill.

Our major funding came from the Social Sciences and Humanities Research Council of Canada, to whom we are grateful. We also received a Humanities Research Grant from McGill University that permitted us to complete research in Ontario.

We would like to thank our extremely dedicated team of research assistants – Sarah Baker, Linda Cohen, Tania Martin, Dahlya Smolash, and Jill Trower – who brought their own expertise to the project and improved it in so many ways. Gretchen Schirmer introduced a remarkable semblance of order into a complex manuscript. David Theodore organized the final illustrations and collected information in Toronto and Kingston. All members of the research team participated in the project's regular meetings, at which many bridges between our disciplines were designed. Such collaboration, we believe, is at the core of feminist research.

All of Canada's provincial architectural associations were extremely cooperative in providing information that was often difficult to obtain. Tim Kehoe of the Royal Architectural Institute of Canada deftly navigated us through the recent reforms that institution has undergone. Several scholars who did preliminary research on Canada's women architects were particularly generous with their own data and offered helpful criticism along the way: these included Mary Clark, Blanche Lemco van Ginkel, and Joan Grierson.

The women architects, registered or not, who provided information for this project are too numerous to thank personally. We hope that their accomplishments will become better known through the publication of this book. It is, in many ways, a tribute to them. We appreciate their interest, their accessibility, and their confidence in us.

We benefited from the opportunity to present our preliminary research at several conferences and in public lectures. These include presentations at Le Colloque sur 'Les jeunes et l'emploi,' Université Laval, February 1996; the 6th International Interdisciplinary Congress on Women, Adelaide, April 1996; the Gender, Work and Organization Conference, Manchester, January 1998; and the Congress of the International Sociological Association, Montreal, July 1998. The public lectures took place at the University of Calgary, the University of British Columbia, the Vancouver Art Gallery, the University of Lincolnshire and Humberside, as well as at McGill. The project was featured on the television show 'Point of View,' aired on the Women's Television Network on 27 March 1995, and was the focus of an article in *La Gazette des femmes* (Stanton 1997). Along these same lines, early versions of chapter 3 appeared as an article in *Recherches féministes* (French) and *Resources for Feminist Research* (English). *The Bulletin of the Society for the Study of Architecture in Canada* and *L'Agenda des femmes 97* published brief versions of certain sections of the work. We are particularly thankful to the Canadian Historical Association, who honoured the project by awarding Annmarie Adams the Hilda Neatby Prize in 1995 for an initial version (in French) of chapter 3.

The feedback we received from interested students, friends, and colleagues throughout the years was crucial to the final direction of the book. Particularly significant was the good advice of Donald Chan, Anne-Marie Daune-Richard, Celia Davies, Carole Després, Françoise Gaudibert, Margaret Gillett, Robert Hill, Peggy Hodges, Nicky Le Feuvre, Andrée Lévesque, Susan Mann, Peter Oberlander, Aurele Parisien, Denise Piché, Maurice Pinard, Vanessa Reid, Gérard Ringon, Norbert Schoenauer, Joan Stelling, Dell Upton, Abby Van Slyck, and Julie Willis. We are especially grateful to Michael Smith for his assistance with the tables in chapter 2 and Appendix B. Kathryn Anthony and Diane Favro provided information on their ongoing research, and the three anonymous reviewers of the manuscript improved the book tremendously. Our warm thanks go to Virgil Duff and Siobhan McMenemy, at the University of Toronto Press, and to Beverley Beetham Endersby, for their professional support of this endeavour. Peta Tancred is grateful to friends in the Razès area of France for their interest and enthusiasm throughout the writing of significant parts of this book. She would also like to thank members of the Groupe Simone of l'Université de Toulouse–Le Mirail for their helpful collaboration during a sabbatical leave in 1995. In more general ways, the Department of Sociology, and particularly the School of Architecture, at McGill University provided countless forms of support for our research.

We would like to express our particular appreciation to our partners, Peter Gossage and Guy Paquette, whose patience with our commitment to this project knew no bounds; their help in a variety of ways has been essential to its accomplishment. Annmarie Adams would like to acknowledge her children, Charlie and Katie, who were born during the course of this research and who contributed indirectly to its completion. We would also like to thank each other; following literally years of collaboration, each of us knows more than she could have imagined to be possible of the discipline of the other – and our friendship endures. We would like to note that, as authors, our names are listed in alphabetical order; we do not consider either of us to be the 'first' author of such a collaborative endeavour.

Annmarie Adams and Peta Tancred
June 1999
Montreal

'DESIGNING WOMEN'

Gender and the Architectural Profession

1

Introduction

This study of women architects within a twentieth-century Canadian framework calls into question the profession's traditional perspective on women members. It demonstrates the extent to which the profession's own definitions and priorities have ignored both women's presence and their widespread contributions to architecture, in two important ways. First, many women architects have made major, unacknowledged contributions to the core areas of the field and, in fact, can be credited with developing and refining innovative and transformatory approaches to practice and design. Second, by refusing on occasion to follow conventional architectural careers, women have branched out into a wide range of alternative employment, ignored by the profession but nevertheless extending and elaborating upon the core areas of architectural practice.

Both the title and the structure of this book are intended to reflect this dynamic relationship between the profession and its women members. As the profession 'designs' women's place within it, women simultaneously 'design' buildings and careers to resist the profession's narrow definition of their role. This tension between the profession and its women members permeates this project.

The book presents the results of an extensive, multiyear research project on Canadian women architects, conducted by an architectural historian and a sociologist. It constitutes an exploration of issues both specific to architecture in Canada and, at the same time, characteristic of many male-dominated workplaces.

'Designing Women' in an International Context

Clearly, Canadian women architects have much in common with their counterparts abroad, and we have profited considerably from the work of our colleagues in various countries who have written about women architects. Studies on U.S. and British women architects were published (and proliferated) as early as the 1970s.[1] In those countries, however, women were accepted as members of the architectural profession much earlier than they were in Canada. Louise Blanchard Bethune registered as a member of the American Institute of Architects in 1888 and Ethel Charles became an architect as early as 1898 in England, but it was not until 1925 that Esther Marjorie Hill was accepted as a member of the Alberta Association of Architects (AAA).[2]

By far, the major part of the research has been done on U.S. women architects, who are the subject of numerous monographs and biographical articles (e.g., Cole 1981, Cole and Taylor 1990). There are, in addition, several scholarly studies of issues specific to women architects in the United States (Kingsley 1988; Wright 1977; Torre 1977) and in Britain (Walker 1984, 1989). These foundation studies tend to be historical (rather than statistical) in their approaches and, without exception, focus on discrimination in the profession. As such, they delineate the woman architect as victim or martyr in an attempt to explain both the relatively small numbers of women architects and their 'limited' contributions to the field. Our study attempts, in many ways, to counter this approach.

There are also many fine studies, let it be said, that look at the contributions women who are untrained in architecture have made to the built environment. These works – the best example is Dolores Hayden's *The Grand Domestic Revolution* (1981) – also focus on Americans and tend to emphasize the power women gained during the Victorian and so-called Progressive era in the United States. Home economist Catharine Beecher, for example, designed a rather radical house in 1869 with her sister, Harriet Beecher Stowe, that was intended to facilitate women's domestic work. Beecher's grand-niece, Charlotte Perkins Gilman, wrote extensively about the home; her 1872 short story 'The Yellow Wallpaper' is a classic tale of women's confinement to the domestic realm. Beecher and Gilman are but two of the women Hayden describes as 'material feminists,' who had made substantial and previously unrecognized contributions to architecture.

New scholarship, we feel certain, will place less emphasis on women's apparent marginalization, and more on their significant and growing presence within the architectural profession. The U.S. scholar Kathryn Anthony, for example, has taken on the challenge of understanding women architects in the context of other minorities. Her recently completed book-length manuscript, entitled 'Shattering the Glass Ceiling: The Role of Gender and Race in the Architectural Profession,' is based on a wide-ranging sample of interviews with U.S. architects.[3]

Outside the United States and Britain, the published work on women architects is scarce. An exhibition to celebrate the fortieth anniversary of the Finnish Association of Women Architects (Architecta) toured Finland in 1982 and resulted in a seventy-two-page catalogue, *Profiles*. At that time, 500 of that country's 1,500 architects were women, and Architecta, when it was founded in 1942, was the first women's architectural association in the world.

Architectural exhibitions, indeed, are a major arena for the dissemination of research on women architects. As did the Finnish example, a number of exhibitions in the United States and Canada have raised public awareness of the contributions of women architects. These highly visible shows, such as 'Women in American Architecture' in 1977, 'That Exceptional One: Women in American Architecture, 1888–1988,' and, in Canada, 'For the Record' in 1986 and 'Constructing Careers' in 1995, highlighted for an interested public the design work of women practitioners. The organization of these exhibitions and the rising number of women students led directly to the formation of many formal and informal associations of women architects.[4]

An Australian scholar, Julie Willis, completed a doctoral dissertation in 1997 titled 'Women in Architecture in Victoria, 1905–1955: Their Education and Professional Life.' Some of her conclusions, in fact, are remarkably similar to ours, perhaps due in no small part to the comparable colonial pasts of Australia and Canada. As in our story, the first woman architect in the state of Victoria, Florence Taylor, qualified as an architect relatively late, in 1902 (registration was not available until 1922). Willis also found little tendency on the part of Australian women architects to specialize in 'women's work,' such as housing and interiors. 'Women architects in Victoria worked in almost every facet of architectural practice, their work experience largely dependent upon their employment situations,' concludes Willis (p. 203). 'There is no evidence to suggest that women architects as a group were marginalised or expected by their employers to be involved in specific types of architectural work or tasks because of their sex' (p. 204). These findings, like ours, contrast sharply with the research on U.S. architects, which has emphasized the pressures placed on the first generation of women architects there to specialize in 'feminine' work.

As Willis also notes in the conclusion to her thesis, however, there are also significant differences in our respective findings.[5] The first Canadian woman architect qualified in 1920, nearly two decades after Taylor. Whereas the numbers of Australian women architects in Victoria were steady and consistent before the Second World War, in Canada there were relatively few registered women architects. Willis underlines the increased difficulties faced by Canadian women in obtaining the office experience necessary for registration, compared with the situation faced by Australian women, suggesting that it may have been a result of 'a high level of distrust of women architects' abilities' (1997, 218). On the other hand, Willis notes the coincidence of women's suffrage with their entry to the profession in both countries.

Although the international literature – apart from these studies on Britain, the United States, Finland, and Australia – is relatively sparse, there are many reasons to be optimistic about future scholarship. In the last few decades, major archives have begun to collect the drawings and papers of women architects. In the United States, for example, the International Archive of Women in Architecture (IAWA) was founded in 1985 to collect the professional papers of women architects. Its Web site (http://scholar2.lib.vt.edu/spec/iawa/iawa. htm) is a rich resource on the subject, offering biographies of women designers, a geographical directory, and links to related sites.

On a much smaller scale but no less significant is the fact that the Canadian Centre for Architecture (CCA), one of the premier architectural archives in the world, has acquired drawings by both van Ginkel and Chard Wisnicki, two of the architects we discuss in chapter 4. In addition, the CCA included in its schedule for the fall 1998 lecture series 'Women in the Practice of Architecture,' highlighting the work of contemporary practitioners: Adele Santos (United States), Sarah Wigglesworth (Britain), Janna Levitt and Brigitte Shim (Canada).

'Designing Women' in the Context of the Professions

In addition to those works that enabled us to locate Canadian women architects within an international context, we have also profited from work on the broader subject of women in the male-dominated[6] professions. Of particular interest have been two bodies of literature: first, a limited literature on women within such professions in the Canadian context; and, second, literature that attempts to theorize the position of women within the male-dominated professions in general.

While the definition of 'profession' may be contested, a generally accepted minimal set of criteria would include the 'monopoly of theoretically grounded knowledge, which in some cases may be guaranteed by law ... Entry into a profession is controlled by examination and the granting of certificates and licences to practice' (Crompton 1987, 420). Sokoloff argues that the core professions are law and medicine, a position that would garner widespread agreement; she classes architecture as an 'established profession,' though her list of the other established professions is a curious one, including, as it does, dentistry, the ministry, and the judicial profession, but also 'science' and 'university teaching,' neither of which can be considered to require 'licences to practice' (1992, 8). As well, she omits engineering, which many would argue easily fulfils the criteria for a profession.

Within this context of the core and established professions, architecture takes its place as a 'modal' profession, in terms both of the proportion of women within its ranks and of the degree of technical knowledge that forms part of the requirements for the profession. On the first point, it is interesting to note that women's presence within architecture, as of 1991,[7] was higher (19 per cent) than in dentistry (15 per cent) or engineering (9 per cent), but significantly lower than in law (29 per cent) or medicine (27 per cent). On the basis of the available literature,[8] it will be interesting to draw additional comparisons as we present the image of women in architecture. On the second point, as architectural historian Kelly Crossman has argued in one of the few historical studies of the development of the profession in Canada, there has been a 'transformation of architecture from a skill rooted in the artistic traditions of western Europe to a profession dependent on the techniques of science and the managerial theories of modern business' (1987, 4).[9]

Of interest in considering women's position within the profession of architecture is their varied relationship to each component domain – namely, art, science, and business. Historically, in none of these fields have women been publicly recognized and vaunted, but their relationship to artistic endeavours has presumed at least an ability to appreciate beauty. On the other hand, women's association with the sciences has been a tenuous one, and it is only recently that they have been recognized as potential participants in business and managerial ranks. Thus, the profession of architecture is located at the crossroads of one of women's potential (believed instinctive) strengths and two domains where women are assumed to be without particular talents. In this sense, the profession presents an interesting conundrum that is not present in the more monolithic professions, and raises the issue of whether the nature of the relevant professional knowledge can contribute to or hinder women's presence within a professional setting.

While this hypothesis has not, to our knowledge, been addressed by other writers on the professions, it does not contradict the existing literature, scant though it may be, which attempts to draw together the studies of women in the professions. This literature is essentially of two kinds: first, certain researchers (e.g., Witz 1992; Crompton 1987) have attempted to 'gender' existing frameworks for the study of the professions in general. For example, Witz, in a very interesting full-length work, attempts to develop a gendered version of what is known as an 'occupational closure approach' to the study of the professions. In essence, Witz argues that the various strategies of professional closure are gendered, with an essentially male exclusionary strategy and a mainly female inclusionary strategy. She also sees that the 'encirclement of women within a related but distinct sphere of competence' (1990, 683) can take place *within* the profession as well as *between* it and related professions. The difficulty with such an approach for this study is twofold: admittedly, Witz offers a possible explanation of how women are kept out of the professions and channelled into certain types of tasks. But how do we explain a situation in which women break through the male-prescribed boundaries? Second, Witz never questions the categories of analysis; for her, the professions are circumscribed bodies, as defined by their mainly male members. Since much of our discussion is concerned with the way that women interrogate the very parameters of the profession, the framework is not very helpful – and this tends to be true of all frameworks that are basically gendered elaborations of traditional approaches.

Instead, we join with some emerging work (Acker 1992; Davies 1996, 1998, forthcoming) that views women in the professions as entrants to yet another workplace organization. In effect, the argument underlines that professions are also ways of organizing work (Davies 1996) and that, in the same way that work organizations do, the professions exhibit an ongoing gendered substructure (Acker 1992). This gendered substructure is the 'congealed dynamic' of ongoing gender relations, at the level of society and within the profession, and it prioritizes the masculinist values that have permeated a male-dominated profession since its inception. Thus, not surprisingly, complex mechanisms are employed to channel women into 'adjunct tasks' (Tancred-Sheriff 1989; see also chapter 3 of this work) within the profession (or sometimes within an adjacent semi-profession). However, given that the gendered substructure is the outcome of ongoing gender relations within the profession, the presence of women puts into question the various masculinist professional practices (chapters 2, 4, and 5 of this study) such that the emerging gendered substructure is in constant flux.

It is in this sense that we talk of the profession 'designing' women and of women 'designing' the profession, for, with the significant entry of women into architecture (and other professions), the underlying and hidden gendered substructure will be modified. However, we have no illusions that this modification will be a rapid one; as we illustrate in chapter 3, the mechanisms through which women are channelled into professionally approved spaces are enormously subtle. As Davies points out (1996, 663), it is not so much that women are *excluded* from professional bodies in the late twentieth century; rather, it is a question of *how* they are included and what particular form that inclusion takes.

As illustrated in this brief discussion, such an approach enables us to view the presence of women within professional parameters from a gendered perspective; that they carry with them new values, new ways of 'doing,' and transformed priorities is by no means surprising. However, we are particularly interested in the extent to which they succeed in imposing these priorities on the professional context and, in so doing, modify the gendered substructure of at least one professional context.

Women's Work within a Male Discourse

One of the difficulties in discussing women's work is that the discussion is necessarily inserted into male 'containers,' since our vocabulary for discussing the workplace has, in the main, been formulated on the basis of men's experience and priorities (Tancred 1995). This is particularly true of women's professional work, since women are entering a domain that has been tightly defined and controlled by their male colleagues. For this reason, a discussion of women within the profession of architecture is usually limited to what *males* have considered to be architectural practice and what has been codified in the rules of membership of the provincial professional associations. As a result, many of women's contributions are neglected and ignored.

As Adams has pointed out in a previous publication (1994a), the considerable architectural activities of many Canadian women have never been recognized by the profession. Sylvia Chaplin, for example, who graduated from McGill University in 1945, was never a member of a provincial professional association (the first woman member was admitted to the Ordre des Architectes du Québec in 1942); she never worked as an architect, despite years of study in the field; and her architectural drawings were never translated into practice.[10] As our research has uncovered, Chaplin is typical of hundreds of Canadian women who functioned outside the male-defined boundaries of the profession. How have these educated-but-never-registered architects coloured our understanding of women's participation in the profession?

The task of uncovering all these 'unregistered professionals'[11] (Clark 1988, 1) is impossible; their numbers are overwhelming, and the relevant sources frequently unavailable. Thus, our study is somewhat constrained by the profession's definition of itself, particularly in our statistical overview. Nevertheless, as will become clear as the discussion proceeds, our early decision to make women (and some men) who exited from provincial associations a major focus of the study has broadened the masculinist definition of the profession to encompass a much wider range of architectural experience. These 'de-registered architects' (see Appendix C: Lexicon) are, by definition, qualified architects who are no longer recognized by their own profession. They are included in our study to provide contemporary examples of the range of work that is undertaken by the unrecognized architect; in effect, we insert our history of women in Canadian architecture into a framework that challenges the profession's definition of its own parameters and locates the profession, instead, within a female-extended discourse.

Architectural historian Abigail Van Slyck noted this same pattern in her insightful review of current research on U.S. women architects in 1992. In discussing the attention paid to the best-known U.S. woman architect, Van Slyck suggested that Julia Morgan attracted such massive scholarly attention because she modelled her career on the norm established by her male colleagues. '[Morgan's] posthumous reward for reinforcing the male norm is a massive biography, produced by a major press, filled with color photographs shot specifically for the publication, and reviewed widely in scholarly journals,' notes Van Slyck (1992, 19). Women who followed less traditional career paths, meanwhile, have attracted relatively little attention. It is the inclusion of such women that differentiates our study from the existing literature. A project that includes every woman who ever studied architecture formally or informally has yet to be undertaken.

The results of our multiple research methods, outlined in Appendix A, are presented in the subsequent chapters. In chapter 2, we raise the issue of an appropriate definition of 'architect.' In Canada, the profession's restricted definition leads to the registration of a very small proportion of women architects, contradicting the significant presence of women that is highlighted by the census. We demonstrate that the 'unregistered professionals' are a very high proportion of all women architects, and that the de-registered architects are also central to the profession, as they elaborate upon and extend the profession's core specializations. This chapter also provides a social scaffolding for our project by recording the presence of women within architecture (and discussing possible explanations for this varying presence) over the total research period, 1920–92.

In chapter 3, we examine how the professional press has depicted women architects, in order to present a coherent image of the profession's view of women. Images of women architects in the press reinforced the exclusivity of the profession in three distinct ways. The *Journal, Royal Architectural Institute of Canada* (hereinafter referred to by its popular title, the *RAIC Journal*) in particular marginalized women's contribution to the design process by focusing on their association with housing and interiors. Advertisements in the journal identified women users of buildings with particular spaces and specific building components, emphasizing their regulation of building details, rather than its overall production; finally, the journal subtly projected an image of the Modern architect in Canada that was quintessentially masculine.

In contrast to this image of women architects in the press, our interviews with many Canadian women architects illuminate the multitude of their contributions, especially towards the development of post-war Modernism.[12] This is the subject of chapter 4, where we examine archival, interview, and portfolio material to develop an image of women's innovations with respect to the Canadian built environment. This more detailed historical study focuses on Ontario and Quebec, Canada's largest provinces. Thus, chapter 4 also offers a comparison of women's roles in these two very different contexts.

Following a brief presentation of available data on women graduates in architecture who have never registered with their provincial associations, interviews with women and men who have de-registered from their provincial association are used to explore influences on, and reasons for, such a decision. In chapter 5 we examine their alternative employment, noting that the vast majority are still working within a broadly defined architectural domain. Gender contrasts are highlighted and reveal a specific pattern of employment for women and men. We conclude that the definition employed by the profession is inadequate for an assessment of women's contributions to architecture.

By way of conclusion, chapter 6 confronts the so-called Quebec question, for both our quantitative and qualitative data indicate that the experiences and roles of Quebec women architects have been distinct in comparison with those of women from other provinces. We argue that the case of Canadian women architects provides good evidence that women tend to come to the fore in times of major social upheavals. We also discuss the so-called Continental model of the professions, which provides greater opportunities for entry through the educational system and, we argue, a wider range of opportunities for practice. Finally, we comment upon the implications of our research for studies of women professionals in general.

We intend this study to contribute to our understanding of the roles of Canadian women architects in its national coverage of the profession, its multidisciplinary approach to the subject, and its redefinition of the 'professional architect.' This last issue, in its broadest terms, has meant that women architects are seen in this research as active agents in their own careers, rather than as mute victims of an uncaring profession. Throughout this study, we have attempted to highlight the innovations and deviations individual women have made relative to their own circumstances rather than in relation to the limitations forced on them by a male-defined profession. As already mentioned, this interplay between the profession and its women members has determined the entire structure of the book. As our chapter titles suggest, two chapters (2 and 3) explore the profession's designs on women and two succeeding chapters (4 and 5) focus on women architects' design and redesign of the profession.

We hope that this book will bring a sense of satisfaction to the generations of women who have already made a difference to architecture in Canada and also encourage young women to consider careers as architects. The next century, we feel certain, will be theirs.

2

Entering Male-Dominated Practice, 1920–1992: The Profession 'Defines' Women Architects

Since we began our study of women in Canadian architecture, a colleague has repeatedly posed the two most basic questions: when, he asks, did women start entering the profession of architecture? and what proportion of the contemporary architectural profession is composed of women? As the project progressed, he became increasingly bemused that we could not provide simple answers to these extremely basic questions.

It is, of course, true that the architectural profession, at the national level, has never maintained data on its membership by gender. The responsibility for collecting such information has remained at the level of the provinces and territories, as each local association came into existence.[1] However, this is not the source of our difficulties in replying to our colleague; after all, we have spent considerable time over the past few years collecting and coordinating such provincial data. In fact, our project has the most complete set of national data on architects in Canada from 1920 to 1992.[2] In that case, why can we not respond to our colleague's questions?

The difficulties stem from problems of definition, which undoubtedly haunt us more than they concern him. To put the matter concretely, what definition of the profession is appropriate for a wide-ranging national study of women architects? Our initial response to this question was a conservative one: as will be discussed shortly, the provincial associations have the responsibility and the legal right to define their profession, and we should follow their undisputed lead in selecting our definition. But a major problem for our study, as suggested in chapter 1, is that association definitions have been formulated by a predominantly male profession and reflect a male perspective on architectural practice. If we wish to articulate women's special contributions to the profession, we would find them hard to delineate within the confines of such male parameters.

We noted a second difficulty with the association definitions. Given the criterion of registering with a provincial association and paying the requisite fee,[3] it would be completely feasible for an individual who possessed *all* necessary qualifications to practise as an architect, but was not formally registered, to be excluded from the definition. For these 'unregistered professionals,'[4] the professional definition is extremely exclusive, based on membership in a mainly male 'club' rather than on any measure of competence.

What other possible definitions are available? Clearly, the Canadian census provides an alternative approach to the profession of architecture, based on subjective information (provided by the individual concerned or a family member) of the nature of architectural work, as interpreted by the census.[5] This definition, needless to say, is much disdained by the professional associations since the legal right to practise as an architect is not included as a criterion. Nevertheless, the census approach is both more subjective and more encompassing; there are clearly a certain number of individuals in Canadian society who describe their work in terms of a certain profession and are so classified by the census. For this reason, the state's definition cannot be set aside in a perfunctory manner and must be accorded due recognition.[6]

In order to reward our colleague for his considerable patience, this chapter provides the full story of women's entry to the architectural profession in Canada. In it, we include both an account from the perspective of the profession, based on data from provincial associations, and an account based on the self-identification of architects, that is, on data obtained from the census. After a brief glance at the professional context of the 1920s, we cover both the pioneering period (1920 to 1970) and the post-pioneering years (1970 to 1992), drawing out the themes characteristic of each. We complete the image with a detailed coverage of registered and unregistered professionals, and of de-registered professionals, including an overview of the post-association employment of this last group. The chapter concludes with an evaluation of our two data sources for an understanding of women architects in Canada.

The Professional Context of the 1920s

As we know from chapter 1, the first Canadian woman to register as an architect joined a provincial association in 1925, and women architects are listed in the Canadian census for the first time as of 1921. Thus, the 1920s were obviously the starting date for women's entry to the profession, however it was defined.

What kind of profession were they entering? In terms of organization, the brief history of the provincial associations is that Ontario and Quebec attained association status in the last decade of the nineteenth century, while the four Western provinces formed architectural associations in the first two decades of the twentieth. The Atlantic provinces' associations were established between 1932 and 1972.[7] Association status usually conferred full professional control on the provincial associations, who were then responsible for delineating the criteria for membership in the profession. Given the decentralization of such control, as Mary Clark points out, 'it is impossible to describe a single set of standards for the registration of architects in Canada' (1988, 1). Her general formulation of requirements, taking into account differences across time and among provinces, is:

> For graduates of Canadian universities, [the requirements] have generally included proof of certain types of post graduate experience, recommendation by a member in good standing, and in many instances exams on various aspects of the profession. For graduates of foreign universities and others entering the profession through the apprenticeship system, additional requirements usually have to be met. (1)

As noted, association status usually meant full control of the profession within a province, but this was not the case in Ontario; while Ontario's professional association dates from 1889, obligatory membership in order to practise architecture dates from the Architects Act of 1931 (Simmins 1989, 106). The Ontario association, in effect, spent four decades fighting for full recognition (Crossman 1987, 47ff.).

At the national level, the Royal Architectural Institute of Canada (RAIC), which was founded to foster closer professional ties across the country and to increase the prestige of the profession, held its first convention in 1907, and the relevant Institute of Architects Bill was approved in 1908, following a stormy passage ('Brief history' 1962, 69ff.). Initially, membership in the RAIC was voluntary, but by 1912 the charter had been amended to make the institute a federation of component provincial associations. However, the RAIC has 'no jurisdiction over its membership in many areas such as education, entrance to the profession, rights of practice, use of the title 'architects,' professional practice, code of ethics and discipline, etc.' (*Interim Report* 1965, 6). These matters were left to the component provincial associations.

Thus, by the date of women's first admission to the architectural profession in Canada, the profession had achieved significant progress. As Crossman points out, by 1910 (and this would be even more true by the 1920s),

> there were now three journals devoted specifically to architecture ... The architect

was now a professional, probably a member of a provincial architectural association and the Royal Architectural Institute of Canada ... While architectural education had been informal and haphazard, by 1910, it was regulated and increasingly
centred in the universities. (1987, 3–4)

Thus, starting in the 1920s, women sought entry to a group that had passed
through the early struggles and had achieved a certain level of organization
and professionalism.

The Pioneering Period, 1920s to 1970

The first Canadian woman registered architect, Esther Marjorie Hill, originally of Guelph, Ontario, became a member of the Alberta Association of
Architects in 1925. Her route to association membership was not an easy one.
She applied to the Alberta Association in 1921 only to have her application
greeted with such 'considerable consternation that [it] led to the requirement
of one year's practical experience after graduation as a condition for membership ...' (Clark 1988, 4; see also Contreras, Ferrara, and Karpinski 1993, 18).
Hill was followed by Alexandra Biriukova, who came from Russia via graduate studies in Rome, and who registered with the Ontario association in 1931,
that is, during the first year that the association controlled provincial membership (see chapter 4 for further details of her career); and by Elma Laird, an
American, who took the comparatively rare apprenticeship route, also registering with the Ontario Association of Architects in 1931.[8] It is interesting
that, of these first three women registrants with provincial associations, two
were immigrants to Canada. They also have in common that they spent extensive periods outside the profession: Hill as a teacher prior to her registration,
and as a journalist, glove-maker, greeting-card designer, and weaver over the
Depression and war period; Biriukova as a nurse from 1934 forward; and
Laird as a secretary after the same date. Clearly, registration with a provincial
association was a necessary but not sufficient step towards architectural
practice.
    If we locate these first three women within the larger picture for the period,
as tables 2.1 and 2.2 demonstrate forty other women joined provincial associations over the next thirty-five years. Following in Hill's footsteps, an
astonishingly high proportion (50 per cent) joined associations in Western
Canada, and nearly the same proportion (47 per cent) of those known to be
educated in Canada attended schools of architecture at the Western universities (UBC, Alberta, and Manitoba). One-third of all these Canadian-educated
women registrants graduated from the University of Manitoba.

TABLE 2.1
Women registrants, by decade of entry into six provincial associations, prior to 1960[a]

Association	1920s	1930s	1940s	1950s	Total
AIBC (BC)	–	1	4	3	8
AAA (AB)	1	1	5	3	10
SAA (SK)	–	–	–	2	2
MAA (MB)	–	–	2	1	3
Subtotal West	1	2	11	9	23 (50%)
OAA (ON)	–	2	5	8	15
OAQ (QC)	–	–	3	5	8
TOTAL	1	4	19	22	46[b] (100%)

[a]Data based on Clark 1988 and material prepared for the 'Designing Women' project from registration records of the Architectural Institute of British Columbia (AIBC), Alberta Association of Architects (AAA), Saskatchewan Association of Architects (SAA), Manitoba Association of Architects (MAA), Ontario Association of Architects (OAA), and the Ordre des architectes du Québec (OAQ).
[b]The actual number of women is 43. Three women registered in two provincial associations prior to 1960. The combinations are: OAA 1950s & AAA 1950s; AAA 1920s & AIBC 1950s; OAA 1940s & AIBC 1940s.

The role of the Western provinces and associations in propelling women into architecture in this early period is an interesting one. We have little material to explain this phenomenon, though an early woman graduate, who moved to Vancouver after a short career in the East, talks about how 'open' the West appeared for practising architects in the 1940s. She goes on to say:

> ... in respect to the residential practice out here [in Vancouver], it was just wonderful because there were clients, everybody was wanting to build after the war, and there was ... oh, I don't know, B.C. at that time had certainly a special kind of almost spiritual quality ... the design climate at that time was sort of lyrical and life-enhancing and extremely unmanipulative ... (F: 23)[9]

Interestingly, Diane Favro documents much the same kind of atmosphere in her work on women architects in early California. As she indicates, 'women in

TABLE 2.2
Women registrants, by decade of entry and university/country of first degree, prior to 1960[a]

University of first degree	1910s–1920s	1930s	1940s	1950s	Total
UBC	–	–	–	1	1
Alberta[h]	–	3	–	–	3
Manitoba	–	2	5	3	10
Subtotal West	–	5	5	4	14 (47%)
Toronto	1	–	3	3	7
McGill	–	–	6	2	8
Beaux Arts	–	–	1	–	1
Subtotal East	1	–	10	5	16 (53%)
Abroad	5	–	4	2	11
TOTAL	6	5	19	11	41[c]

[a]Data based on Clark 1988, Figure 3, and material prepared for the 'Designing Women' project from registration records of the AIBC, AAA, SAA, MAA, OAA, and OAQ.
[b]Note that the School of Architecture of the University of Alberta closed in 1939. The next university in Alberta to have a school of architecture was the University of Calgary; this opened in 1972.
[c]The actual number of women is 43. One woman studied in two schools and is thus double-counted in this table; one woman followed the apprenticeship route; and there are two women for whom we have no information.

the freewheeling atmosphere of California at the turn of the century found their services readily accepted in a variety of fields' (1991, 48–9). While she is discussing an earlier period than the one covered by our data, her emphasis on a 'frontier mentality' that provided freedom from 'confining stereotypes' (1992, 118) coincides with the comments of our Vancouver architect and suggests a pioneering interpretation – that women breaking into a male-dominated profession do so more easily in an environment that both needs professionals and is open to new ideas and influences.[10]

As for the University of Manitoba's influence over early women graduates in architecture, a list of all its instructors in architecture through the 1940s and 1950s shows that no fewer than four women were on the faculty at that time (of whom two were themselves graduates of the University of Manitoba, and two others of U.S. institutions).[11] Their presence may have been linked to the founding at the University of Manitoba of the first course in interior decoration in Canada (see chapter 3). Given that few *current* schools of architecture could boast such a female presence,[12] it is worth hypothesizing that these women instructors were important influences on the presence of registered women architects.

Our three earliest registered women architects also remind us of the potential influence of immigrants on women's professional access. This factor has been explored for the professions in general (Boyd 1975; Denis 1981; Ng 1987), but is rarely mentioned for architecture in particular, though Andrea Dean, in an article on U.S. women architects, makes glancing reference to the high percentage of women principals born and educated abroad (1982, 42). Has immigrant women's presence within Canadian architecture been sufficiently influential to provide a role model for other women? If we take a quantitative approach to this question in the present chapter,[13] table 2.2 shows that over one-quarter of the pioneers who entered the provincial associations before 1960 were educated abroad. While we do not have complete information on place of birth and education for registrants from all provinces, additional material is available from the Architectural Institute of British Columbia (AIBC), who were particularly helpful in providing data. From tables B.5 and B.6 (Appendix B), it is interesting to note that 77 per cent of early entrants (up to the end of the 1960s) were born abroad, and 54 per cent of them were educated abroad.[14] These tables also show that these proportions are much higher for the 'pioneering' era than they are for the period from 1970 forward.[15]

Obviously, one cannot generalize from data for one or two provinces with a particular pattern of immigration to the experience of all women architects. Nevertheless, the proportions for the early period in British Columbia are so high that one can put forward the reasonable hypothesis that women immigrants' contributions to the field, both numerically and as potential role models, were extremely important among women who first registered by the end of the 1960s.

As we see, the pre-1970 period was a special one for the registered architects of Canada. Their slow rate of entry to the provincial associations is evident; the influence of Western Canadian education and practice comes through in the pattern of registration; and the contribution of immigrant women in this early period must be underlined.

The Post-Pioneering Years, 1970–1992

What is the picture for registered architects if we include the post-1970 period? Details of the registration of all women and men architects prompt the following observations (table B.7). First, we are dealing with a fairly small profession (slightly more than 11,000 registrants between 1920 and 1992),[16] of whom 9.3 per cent were women. Second, as we know, the proportion of women registrants increased *very* slowly between 1920 and 1970; it doubled during the 1970s, nearly tripled during the 1980s, and continued to increase significantly during the early 1990s. In effect, the 1970s constitute a watershed for the entry of women into Canadian architectural associations.

Third, Quebec stands out, with respect to the pattern of entry to its architectural association. While most of the provinces indicate that women entered around 5–9 per cent of registered architect positions for the period overall, in Quebec a total of 16 per cent of all registrants were women. Given that Quebec's women architects did not start registering until the 1940s, there has been considerable catching up over the succeeding decades. Particularly in the 1980s (25 per cent) and early 1990s (37 per cent) Quebec shows very high percentages of new women registrants, figures that are not even approached by those for the other provinces over the same period.

If we turn next to a 'snapshot' of the profession for the post-1960 period, that is, an image of membership in the provincial associations over time (table B.8), we note that, as of 1992, 11.5 per cent of registered Canadian architects were women. Most provinces record the number of women members as between 4 per cent and just over 9 per cent of total membership, but, once again, Quebec stands out against this pattern, with 18 per cent women members in 1992, a proportion that more than doubled between 1981 and 1991.

The specificity of the Quebec pattern is, of course, a conundrum that is reproduced in a variety of arenas. Unfortunately, we have no qualitative data on current Quebec registered women architects (in contrast to those in other provinces) that might help us to 'solve' the conundrum.[17] In chapter 6, we deal with this question in greater detail, putting forward hypotheses to explain the unique aspects of women's presence within the Quebec architectural profession.

Before we leave our data on registered architects, there is one question that should be examined more closely: Are women maintaining their registration as architects at approximately the same rate as their male colleagues are? This is an important question, and we address it in greater detail in the section on the de-registered professionals. However, the data that answer this specific question are to hand and merit our attention. Thus, if we posit a 'normal' career of about thirty years for professional architects,[18] the additional calculations at the bottom of table B.7 show that 11.3 per cent of registrants for the thirty-two-year period from 1960 to 1992 were women. If we turn to table B.8, we note that, as of 1992, 11.5 per cent of registered architects were women, that is, a proportion just slightly higher than expected for women entrants to the profession in the relevant career period. Thus, these data demonstrate that, for the whole profession, women are maintaining their registration in architectural associations at about the same rate as are their male colleagues.

Association data have allowed us to respond to the basic questions about women as registered architects. We now know that women started to register in the mid-1920s and that, after a slow rate of entry up to the 1970s, which was assisted by the Western provinces and universities and by the contribution of immigrant women, they increased their presence to a proportion of 11.5 per cent by 1992. We have noted the particularity of the Quebec pattern – late entry, starting in the 1940s, but overtaking all other provinces by 1992. Finally, association data do *not* support the assumption that more women cease to be association members than do their male colleagues.

Registered and Unregistered Professionals

We turn now to data on registered and unregistered professionals, recognizing that the census definition employed is a subjective one. As can be seen from table B.9, the census indicates a slightly earlier entry date for women architects: as of 1921 (the first census year that women are mentioned), 0.3 per cent, or a maximum of 4 out of 1,169, Canadian architects were women. The pattern of growth in women's presence, however, is much the same as for registered architects only – a slow increase up to the 1970s, when the proportion of women doubles; during the 1980s, the percentage more than doubles, and it reaches 19.1 per cent by 1991. While the pattern of growth may be similar, it should be noted from a comparison of tables B.8 and B.9 that the census indicates a significantly higher proportion of women architects in each decade, from 1961 forward and, as of 1991, the census shows the proportion of women (19.1 per cent) to be nearly *double* that indicated for the provincial associations (10.6 per cent). Clearly, the census is not only more inclusive in its overview of the profession (it cites a profession of about 12,000, as opposed to 7,500 registered architects), but the definition employed is particularly inclusive of women, as compared with men.

If we look at data for the provinces, Quebec is the major exception to the provincial pattern, for census data exhibit a pattern for Quebec that is similar to the one highlighted by provincial association statistics. Quebec records a low proportion of women from the 1940s[19] to the 1970s, and then starts doubling the proportion over the 1970s and through the 1980s, attaining a comparatively high proportion, 25 per cent by 1991.

On the basis of background material on all those working in architecture (cf. tables B.10–B.16), it can be seen that the main contrasts between the genders is that the woman architect is younger and slightly more likely to hold a university degree; despite such qualifications, she is more likely to have a fragmented and tenuous connection to the labour force, in terms of less full-time work and fewer weeks of work, than her male colleague. She is also slightly more likely to be salaried (rather than self-employed)[20] than he is. As suggested by the high proportion of women architects in Quebec, she is more likely to be francophone than her male colleague; and, finally, she is significantly more likely to be single, as is true of many professional women as they struggle with the 'double day' of work, though this may also reflect the relatively young age of women architects.

What about the role of immigrant women architects? Are the results the same if we include unregistered as well as registered architects? If we turn to table B.17, the proportion of women and men architects, as of 1991, who were born abroad is similar (30 per cent and 36 per cent). Table B.18 documents the period of immigration for both women and men architects, which tends to reflect the more recent entry of women to the profession. Data not included in Appendix B indicate that, if we look at trends over time, 1981 is the first year when country of origin was similar for women and men. Prior to this date, the overall proportion of women immigrants is higher (over 50 per cent) than for men, and their country of origin is Europe only.[21] In brief, the data support the material presented on registered architects, that is, that the contribution of immigrant women architects was particularly important in the 'pioneering' period, while, from the 1970s forward, the variety of national backgrounds decreases, and the countries of origin become very similar for women and men.

We now have a broader set of responses for our colleague's questions. Following the registration of the first woman architect in 1925, women, as of 1992, represented 11.5 per cent of registered architects (10.6 per cent in 1991). But, if we include both registered and unregistered architects, a few women worked as architects prior to 1921 and, as of 1991, they constituted 19.1 per cent of those who define their work as being within the architectural field. As can be seen, each data source paints a very different image of women in architecture; perhaps our colleague can now understand why a succinct, hastily provided response to his questions posed more of a challenge than he had anticipated.

Our two data sources provide an opportunity to contrast the image for registered professionals with that obtained for both registered and unregistered professionals. Tables 2.3A and 2.3B present the comparisons for two dates: in 1991 (when the census includes a wider range of specializations than do association data) and 1961 (when the definition for the two data sources is identical; cf. note 6).

TABLE 2.3A
Women architects, by province, as a percentage of total architects, according to 1991 census data[a] and 1991 provincial association (PA) data[b]

	BC	AB	SK	MB	ON	QC	NB	NS	PE	NF	Canada
Census	11.6%	18.8%	11.8%	9.8%	17.9%	25.0%	11.8%	13.0%	–	–	19.1%
(N =)	(1805)	(850)	(85)	(205)	(4365)	(4025)	(85)	(270)	(25)	(65)	(11,810)
PA	7.2%	6.8%	3.0%	4.6%	8.6%	16.6%	3.2%	6.9%	–	–	10.6%
(N =)	(1052)	(585)	(133)	(328)	(2511)	(2623)	(93)	(188)	(16)	(38)	(7567)

TABLE 2.3B
Women architects, by province, as a percentage of total architects, according to 1961 census data[c] and 1961 provincial association (PA) data[d]

	BC	AB	SK	MB	ON	QC	NB	NS	PE	NF	Canada
Census	2.2%	3.0%	1.4%	1.6%	1.8%	2.9%	–	2.0%	–	–	2.2%
(N =)	(321)	(197)	(73)	(183)	(1138)	(921)	(34)	(50)	(6)	(12)	(2940)
PA	1.2%	3.8%	1.7%	0.7%	1.1%	0.9%	–	–	–	–	1.2%
(N =)	(251)	(157)	(58)	(148)	(982)	(692)	(26)	(52)	(0)	(16)	(2382)

[a]From the 1991 census (Cat. no. 93-327). A 'random rounding' of all figures to multiples of 5 by Canada census affects the totals.
[b]Data prepared for the 'Designing Women' project based on: (i) registration records of the AIBC, AAA, SAA, MAA, OAA, OAQ, AANB, NSAA, AAPEI, and the NAA; and (ii) Royal Architectural Institute of Canada (RAIC) archival material.
[c]From the 1961 Census Trend Report (Cat. no. 98-551-LS-1).
[d]Data prepared for the 'Designing Women' project based on: (i) registration records of the AIBC, AAA, SAA, MAA, OAA, OAQ, AANB, NSAA, AAPEI, and the NAA; and (ii) Royal Architectural Institute of Canada (RAIC) archival material.

To take the situation in 1991 to start with, we note that unregistered professionals represent 36 per cent of all those who describe their work as within the architectural field.[22] However, table 2.3A also shows indirectly that the proportion of women unregistered professionals is significantly higher than the percentage of men in the same situation.[23] In effect, as of 1991, we estimate that 64 per cent of women who describe themselves as architects do not register with provincial associations, as compared with 29 per cent of the men.[24] Linked to this observation is the fact that the proportion of women is always higher when we include both registered and unregistered professionals.

If we turn to the comparisons in 1961, with identical definitions, as might be anticipated the extent of the differences between the two data sources is less marked, and we have only 19 per cent more architects than are registered with provincial associations. In effect, the inclusion of a much wider range of specializations in 1991 would seem to be an important factor in accounting for contrasts between the two categories of architect. This said, even with identical definitions, there are 558 more architects than registered professionals as of 1961.

But the contrasting results in 1961, for women and men separately, are of considerable interest. In effect, 55 per cent of women working in the architectural field were not registered with provincial associations, in contrast with 18 per cent of the men. The identity of definition in 1961 diminishes the proportion of men unregistered professionals significantly, while the proportion of women remains astonishingly high. This suggests that the greater range of specializations is a major explanation for the higher number of men architects as opposed to registered architects, while, for the women, the range of specializations is a minor factor, and their unregistered status must be based on alternative explanations.

What these explanations might be is, of course, a matter for further exploration. However, at this early point, two hypotheses can be put forward: (a) that a higher proportion of women than men never register with provincial associations following their architectural education, for whatever reason; and/or (b) that a higher proportion of women than men de-register from provincial associations.[25]

To provide a definitive answer as to whether qualified women are more reluctant than men to register with provincial associations (the first hypothesis), we would have to trace a representative cohort of female and male graduates in architecture through their subsequent careers, particularly their registration experience. This would be a major undertaking, and, unfortunately, could not be included in the present research project.[26] However, we do have illustrative data that suggest some preliminary conclusions on this topic.

Mary Clark, for example, in her partial study of Canadian women architects, argues that 'the proportion of women graduates who have registered appears to have been much lower than for male graduates.' She goes on to document that, 'of the twenty-seven Ontario women graduates [between 1920 and 1960], only half became registered architects' (1988, 1). Our records, more complete than those of Clark, suggest that a maximum of one-third of Ontario women graduates actually registered during this period.[27]

Whether we use Clark's estimate or our own calculations, it is clear that a high proportion of women graduates in architecture, at least in Ontario, were excluded from association data up to 1960. This finding appears to be reasonable for the pioneering period, if only because of the hesitant attitude of provincial associations towards the registration of women. However, while one could hypothesize that this gender difference has continued into the more recent period in muted form, we really need additional data to draw firm conclusions. The possibility remains, however, that one of the reasons for a higher proportion of women unregistered professionals arises from the greater tendency of qualified women graduates to be 'never-registered professionals.'

As to the second hypothesis – that women 'exit' provincial associations at a greater rate than do their male colleagues – it is worth noting that there is a considerable literature to support such an explanation. The most wide-ranging study is that of Jacobs (1989), who found that, of a national sample of 3,762 U.S. women who were employed over the period 1967–77, 'for every 100 women in male-dominated occupations who were employed in two consecutive years ... the revolving door sends 10 out for every 11 it lets in' (p. 4). While Jacobs does not compare the rates for women and men, the figures cited are intriguing, particularly since the feminist literature has long been grappling with the slow increase in the presence of women in a wide range of male-dominated occupations.

The second particularly relevant set of data comes from Hagan and Kay (1995), who studied the work histories of Ontario women and men lawyers. They conclude that there is a higher proportion of women than men who are not practising law, as measured by data on the first five professional positions held (the average number of positions is below 2.5 for both women and men). They also note that women are more likely to go into government employment (1995, table 5.2). They conclude that there is an 'overrepresentation of women among those lawyers leaving the practice of law' (p. 114). While these data have been cited to support the contention that women are leaving a male-dominated profession faster than men, in fact all they indicate is that, by the fourth position held, there is the strongest contrast in the proportion of highly mobile Ontario women and men who are not practising law – and this difference *decreases* by the fifth position held. Thus, the authors' own data suggest that at least the extent of the difference could well be a temporary phenomenon; there is certainly no evidence to indicate whether or not the women (and men) concerned have definitively left the profession of law.

As far as women architects are concerned, could a high rate of exit from provincial associations explain their considerable presence as unregistered professionals? Do they, in fact, exit such associations at a greater rate than men? From the data presented in this chapter, we know that women and men leave[28] provincial associations, for whatever reasons, at approximately the same rate. Unless we hypothesize that more men than women leave for reasons other than de-registration, that is, die during their careers (unlikely), tend to retire earlier (also unlikely, see the next section), or become members of associations outside Canada (possible), then women are exiting from provincial associations at about the same rate as men.[29]

De-registered Professionals

What, in fact, is the rate of de-registration for women architects? Fortunately, this question can be addressed directly as our research methodology included tracing *every* woman who had ever entered a Canadian architectural association between 1920 and 1992 over her subsequent career (see Appendix A). Table 2.4 shows the number of women registering in, and exiting, mobile, retired, or deceased from the ten Canadian architectural associations, and provides totals for women leaving, by province. As can be seen, of the 1,057 women registrants, about one-eighth (11.8 per cent) had exited over the research period; this rate will, of course, increase as the younger women have further opportunities to de-register. Retirement and death account for a minimal proportion of those who have ceased to be members of provincial associations. Thus, the total, but still preliminary rate for women leaving these associations is 19.0 per cent.[30]

It is possible to compare departure rates over time so that we can assess if they are increasing or diminishing, but the conclusions to be drawn can only be provisional. Tables B.19 and B.20 provide information on registrants, by decade of entry and by way of leaving, for both the Ontario Association of Architects and the Ordre des Architectes du Québec.[31] The only decades for which data can be considered 'complete' are the 1930s, 1940s, and 1950s (i.e., allowing for a career of about thirty years) for which the exit rates are 33.3 per cent (OAA) and 37.5 per cent (OAQ), though in both instances the relevant number of registrants is very low. When we consider the 1960s and 1970s, the career period is, of course, incomplete; thus the exit rates of 13 (OAA) and

TABLE 2.4
Women registrants and those leaving provincial associations between 1925 and 1992[a]

Province	No. women registrants	No./% women exiting[b]	No./% women mobile[c]	No./% women retiring[d]	No./% women deceased[e]	Total no./% women leaving[f]
BC	107	11	6	2	2	21
		10.3	5.6	1.9	1.9	19.6
AB	58	11	7	2	3	23
		19.0	12.1	3.4	5.2	39.7
SK	9	4	2	0	0	6
		44.4	22.2			66.7
MB	24	5	3	1	0	9
		20.8	12.5	4.2		37.5
ON	277	23	14	10	3	50
		8.3	5.1	3.6	1.1	18.1
QC	556	67	9	4	3	83
		12.1	1.6	0.7	0.5	14.9
NB	8	2	1	0	0	3
		25.0	12.5			37.5
NS	16	1	2	1	0	4
		6.3	12.5	6.3		25.0
PE	2	1	1	0	0	2
		50.0	50.0			100
NF	0	0	0	0	0	0
Total	1057	125	45	20	11	201
		11.8	4.3	1.9	1.0	19.0

[a]Data prepared for the 'Designing Women' project from: (i) registration records of the AIBC, AAA, SAA, MAA, OAA, OAQ, AANB, NSAA, AAPEI, and the NAA; and (ii) Royal Architectural Institute of Canada (RAIC) archival material.
[b]Exiting is defined as: (i) leaving the provincial association entirely; or (ii) moving to a status which does not permit calling oneself 'architect' (i.e., associate status in some provinces); or (iii) retiring 'early'; that is, prior to thirty years of practice or prior to retirement age.
[c]Mobile is defined as resigning altogether; or resigning to associate status from one provincial association and subsequently reregistering in another province; or resigning from one provincial association while retaining membership in another.
[d]Retiring is defined as either resigning or retiring (depending on provincial protocol) from a provincial association: (i) after at least 30 years' practice or (ii) at retirement age.
[e]Deceased is used to refer to women whose membership was terminated solely because they had died. This category does not include women who passed away subsequent to leaving a provincial association.
[f]Leaving is the sum total of all four ways of ceasing to be a member of a provincial association.

27 per cent (OAQ) are likely to increase, given that the women involved still have some years of working experience before them. It remains to be seen whether the decreasing exit rates for the most recent registrants presage lower rates for the future, though both cohorts have had very little career time for such rates to be valid. What is clear is that the OAQ demonstrates higher exit rates both for the overall period and for the subperiods delineated.

A second method of looking at trends over time is to compare the exit rate of registrants of various decades who have a similar length of service. This facilitates comments on the actions of cohorts with similar experience who entered at different periods. Tables 2.5A and 2.5B provide data, once again for the two largest associations, on women who exited their associations after a specific period of service.[32] A curious pattern emerges for both associations when we contrast entrants from earlier and later periods. In effect, the later women registrants tend to leave earlier in their careers; OAA data show that nearly 55 per cent of post-1970 registrants who exited did so within the first five years of their careers, while this was true for only 38 per cent of exiters from the earlier period. The contrast is even stronger (and the N higher) for the OAQ; 55.5 per cent of later entrants who exited did so with up to five years of service, whereas *none* of the earlier registrants who exited did so with fewer than five years of service. It appears that the pioneering women architects took longer to decide to exit from their associations.[33] Given that the data for the latest entrants are incomplete, the precise percentage of women who exit could be modified in the future. However, the contrasts are so strong, particularly for the OAQ, that it is possible to assert that later registrants are taking decisions about de-registration earlier in their careers.

What can we conclude about women who de-register from provincial associations? First, the preliminary rate of de-registration, for all women registrants for the period 1920–92, is 11.8 per cent. Whether or not such a rate is 'too high' is for the provincial associations to judge; they may well be concerned about losing at least one-eighth of their women members over the course of their careers. This rate of de-registration could be a matter of even greater concern if we remember that the rates appear to be similar for women and men. If we look at completed rates for the two largest provincial associations, between one-third and nearly two-fifths of early women registrants (prior to 1960) exited their associations during the course of their careers.

As to changes over time, the rate of exit may be decreasing within the two largest associations, though this is hard to judge, given the incomplete nature of the data on later entrants. The Quebec association continues to demonstrate a higher rate of exits for the overall period, and particularly for the subperiods delineated.

TABLE 2.5A
Women exiting the OAA, by cohort and years of service prior to departure, 1930–1989[a]

Year reg'd	Number of women exiting after a specified number of years										
	0–2	3–5	6–8	9–11	12–14	15–17	18–20	21–3	24–6	27–9	Total
1930–4		1									1
1935–9											0
1940–4											0
1945–9					1						1
1950–4		2					1				3
1955–9											0
1960–4				1							1
1965–9			2								2
Total *1930–69*	0	3 37.5%	2 25%	1 12.5%	1 12.5%	0	1 12.5%	0	0	0	8
1970–4	1	1						1			3
1975–9					2						2
1980–4	1		1								2
1985–9	1	2			1						4
Total *1970–89*	3 27.3%	3 27.3%	1 9.1%	0	3 27.3%	0	0	1 9.1%	0	0	11
TOTAL	3 15.8%	6 31.6%	3 15.8%	1 5.3%	4 21.1%	0	1 5.3%	1 5.3%	0	0	19

[a]Shaded cells indicate that these cells are not complete; that is, women exiting post-1992 could be added later. Please note that this table includes only women who registered prior to 1990; therefore, the total of women exiting does not correspond to the total in table B.19.

TABLE 2.5B
Women exiting the OAQ, by cohort and years of service prior to departure, 1940–1989[a]

Year reg'd	Number of women exiting after a specified number of years										
	0–2	3–5	6–8	9–11	12–14	15–17	18–20	21–3	24–6	27–9	Total
1940–4											0
1945–9			1								1
1950–4										1	1
1955–9					1						1
1960–4				1				2		1	4
1965–9									1		1
Total 1940–69	0	0	1 12.5%	1 12.5%	1 12.5%	0	0	2 25%	1 12.5%	2 25%	8
1970–4				2		1	1				4
1975–9	2	5	2		3	2					14
1980–4	2	4	7	2							15
1985–9	8	9	4								21
Total 1970–89	12 22.2%	18 33.3%	13 24.1%	4 7.4%	3 5.6%	3 5.6%	1 1.9%	0	0	0	54
TOTAL	12 19.4%	18 29.0%	14 22.6%	5 8.1%	4 6.5%	3 4.8%	1 1.6%	2 3.2%	1 1.6%	2 3.2%	62

[a]Shaded cells indicate that these cells are not complete; that is, women exiting post-1992 could be added later. Please note that this table includes only women who registered prior to 1990; therefore, the total of women exiting does not correspond to the total in table B.20.

Finally, there is a strong suggestion that post-1970 women registrants, at least in the two largest provincial associations, who decide to exit their provincial associations do so at an earlier career stage than do their pioneering colleagues. This may also be cause for concern for provincial associations; not only are they losing at least one-eighth of their female membership, but they are losing such members earlier.

Leaving aside the potential concerns of provincial associations, from the point of view of this study the data on exits from provincial associations lead us in certain directions and raise further queries. Apart from arguing that deregistration is not a major reason for the particularly high proportion of unregistered women professionals, we are also interested in whether or not these qualified architects continue to work in the architectural field. What happens to the de-registered woman professional? And, specifically, do we continue to include her as a working architect who contributes to the profession, or is her subsequent career of little interest to the practice of architecture? Answering these questions will help us to respond to the question of definition that was raised earlier in this chapter.

Where Do They Go?

Within the profession of architecture, it is widely recognized that registration is not essential for the practice of the craft. Mary Clark points out, for example, that registration,

> is not mandatory for certain aspects of architectural practice. Graduates of architectural programs can work their way into positions of considerable responsibility under registered architects in private practice or public sector architectural departments, and occasionally have become silent partners or shareholders in large architectural firms. They can become educators, researchers or volunteer members of professional committees and juries. Others develop their own practices based on small-scale residential and commercial projects that are not the sole domain of registered architects under provincial building codes. (1988, 1)[34]

In keeping with this assessment, the Royal Architectural Institute of Canada has recently recognized that 'there is a significant percentage of graduates from the Schools of Architecture who, today, are not going into traditional practice or, for one reason or another, are working in architectural practice but have chosen not to become registered.'[35] As a result of this recognition, the by-laws of the institute were modified in 1994 to include as full members not only those who are or have been registered with provincial associations, but also those with relevant educational qualifications or who hold an academic appointment at a Canadian university school of architecture. However, as pointed out earlier, the RAIC is not the *licensing* association for practising architects, but rather 'a voluntary organization and a forum for developing and sharing the quality of architecture.'[36] While the RAIC recognition of a wider range of qualifications is symbolic of a possibly more flexible stance on the part of the profession towards new forms of architectural practice, there is no evidence so far that the provincial licensing bodies are ready to follow suit and to recognize 'unofficial practice.'

While neither Clark nor the RAIC cites actual examples of such 'unofficial practice,' our interviews with a sample of de-registered architects, both women and men, enable us to document their post-association employment in specific terms. As indicated in Appendix A, we interviewed thirty-seven de-registered architects, twenty-seven women from across Canada, from Quebec to British Columbia, and ten men from Quebec only. Included within the information obtained was an overview of each architect's career.

We were struck by the post-association employment of the women architects interviewed, noting that about four-fifths *at some time* used their architectural qualifications despite lapsed association registration, and around three-quarters *always* used these qualifications in post-association employment; that is, they never worked in fields that had no link[37] with architecture.

What were these types of occupations? Additional information available in table 2.6 shows that one of the most important areas of employment was architecture itself, where about one-fifth of the women worked in 'unofficial' architectural practice – with a family firm, as consultants, as project managers, as advisers, or as independent architects. This kind of post-association employment is, of course, facilitated by the very elitist definition of the profession espoused by the provincial architectural associations, for finally one needs the architect's 'stamp' only if one is responsible for signing drawings;[38] in the present context of multi-person architectural firms, arrangements can be made so that only one or two architects need to register – and a vast amount of architectural work is carried out by non-registered architects. Another major area of post-association employment was teaching in architecture-related fields, mainly at the college level, where nearly one-fifth of our women ex-registrants taught in design, civil engineering, and interior design; a couple of women taught art at the primary/secondary level.

Slightly smaller groups were employed in urban planning or the arts, where they worked as project managers in art galleries or museums, or as independent artists. Given that drawing is a major part of architectural education, this result is not very surprising. Finally, there remains a list of idiosyncratic

TABLE 2.6
Occupational destinations of the sample of de-registered architects

Type of occupation	All women	Quebec women	Quebec men
Architecture – unofficial practice	5 (19%)	3 (17%)	5 (42%)
Teaching in architecture – related fields	5 (19%)	4 (22%)	1 (8%)
Urban planning	3 (11%)	3 (17%)	1 (8%)
Arts	2 (7%)	–	–
Construction	–	–	2 (17%)
Miscellaneous	6 (22%)	4 (22%)	–
Non-architectural employment	6 (22%)	4 (22%)	3 (25%)
TOTAL	27[a] (100%)	18[b] (100%)	12[c] (100%)

[a]The actual number of women is 27. Two women were still pursuing further studies at the time of the interviews and are excluded; two women are included within two categories.
[b]The actual number of women is 19. Two women were still pursuing further studies and are excluded; one woman is included within two categories.
[c]The actual number of men is 10. One man was still pursuing further studies and is excluded; three men are included within two categories.

employment, where over one-fifth of the women used their background to expand markets for construction products; to develop software related to architecture; to work as journalists specializing in the architectural field; or to be associated with the construction of public sculpture, or with real estate or housing developments as managers or bookkeepers. While such employment would undoubtedly be rejected by the provincial associations as architectural occupations, strictly speaking one can distinguish the links between a background in architecture and these occupations.

Thus, of the women who have withdrawn from architectural associations, an overwhelming majority have translated their architectural qualifications into some form of related employment. Phrased in this way, the observation is almost commonplace; the women would be negating their qualifications at the tertiary level were they to do otherwise. Nevertheless, the professional associations are not prepared to recognize most of such post-association employment as legitimate architectural work, even when, as occurs in some cases, individuals are occupying the identical position, and carrying out identical work, during and after their association membership. And presumably this explains, to some degree, the significant proportion of women architects, on the basis of census data, who are not registered architects according to the associations.

But, one might well ask, would these observations not also hold true of male colleagues who have decided not to continue their association membership? Fortunately, we anticipated this question and, as mentioned earlier, we interviewed a small sample of men, from one province (Quebec). The overall results are similar for Quebec women and men;[39] about three-quarters of the women and men used their architectural qualifications in some manner in their post-association employment, and nearly 80 per cent of the Quebec women (as compared with 70 per cent of the men) used their qualifications in *all* their subsequent employment (information not included in table 2.6). The men who withdrew from their associations worked primarily in two areas – first, in a form of architectural employment which did not require registration, and, second, in construction; only one man had experience of teaching, at the college level (in computer drafting), and one had worked in urban planning.[40] While the Quebec women and men have a similar level of non-architectural employment, it appears that the men are more present in the unofficial practice of architecture and in construction than are the women, who undertake a wider gamut of employment.

In chapter 5, we look in greater detail at the this group of de-registered architects, outlining the reasons that these men and women moved to post-association status. For the moment, it is sufficient to underline that the vast majority of both women and men de-registered architects worked at some time, and, in the main, throughout their subsequent careers, in what could be conceptualized as an extended architectural domain, that is, one that was linked to their architectural qualifications. As we argue even more forcefully in chapter 5, the women seem to have reacted with particular ingenuity by seeking out innovative areas of work that make use of their architectural expertise.

Conclusion

Let us return to our colleague's concerns with respect to women architects. In some ways, our two data sources provide parallel information on women in Canadian architecture. In the case of both registered architects and architects in general, women entered the profession around the 1920s and, following a watershed in 1970, increased their presence significantly into the 1990s. In both cases, there is agreement that the presence – and thus potential influence – of immigrant women was particularly marked in the pre-watershed period. In both cases, there is a distinct pattern of entry in Quebec; that is, women in that province entered late, but extremely rapidly, thus easily overtaking the proportion of women registered architects in the other provinces by the 1990s.

The points on which the two approaches disagree include the absolute size of the profession. As we have noted, there are significantly more architects than registered architects. At the same time, the category 'architect' is much more inclusive of *women* than is that of 'registered architect'; in effect, the census data show nearly double the proportion of women in 1991 as do association data, thus underlining the very high proportion of unregistered women professionals.

Our discussion of unregistered professionals indicates not only that they are numerous – over one third of those working in the architectural field – but also that women working as architects are much *more* likely to be unregistered (nearly two-thirds) rather than registered professionals. Thus, the exclusion of the unregistered professional from any discussion of architectural practice neglects a wide range of women's contributions, while misrepresenting, to a lesser extent, the presence of men.

We have also learned, from a comparison of architects and registered architects in both 1961 and 1991, that, while an important proportion of male unregistered professionals are located in specializations that are not officially recognized by the associations, this is not as true of women. This finding may be somewhat surprising since women's association with landscape architecture (unrecognized by the profession) might have been considered to explain to some extent their considerable presence among unregistered architects. In fact, it is the men unregistered professionals who extend the architectural domain by working in unrecognized specializations, while the reason for the high proportion of women unregistered professionals lies elsewhere.

We conclude that, as far as women are concerned, the current association definitions are inadequate instruments for appreciating women's contributions to the field of architecture. While we are not frequent admirers of state-developed definitions for women's experience, we must acknowledge that the census definition, which includes the never-registered and de-registered professional, as well as a wider range of specializations, is a preferable container for appreciating women's, and thereby all, architectural work. It may not be the perfect container, as that would be rooted in the major preoccupations which guide the current research and remain to be translated into definitional terms. But a non-association definition of the profession is clearly preferable.

3

Images in the Mirror:
The Profession's Perspective on
Women Architects

Ebba Nilsson always wanted to be an architect.[1] Growing up in Waterville, Quebec, she watched with interest as her father, David Nilsson, a Swedish immigrant, worked as a carpenter on the town's Congregational church, constructed cottages in nearby North Hatley, and built a number of barns in the Eastern Townships region. Upon graduation from the Waterville Model School, Ebba went off to Philadelphia to study architecture for three years, working as a mother's helper and tutoring young children to support her studies. When Ebba returned to Waterville in 1932, however, she began a long career in teaching rather than architecture. She was ten years too early; it was not until 1942 that a woman first registered in Quebec as a professional architect.[2]

As we noted in the introduction to this book, we know relatively little about the emergence of women architects in Canada, relative to women architects in the United States and Britain, or of the contributions of never-registered women to the profession of architecture.[3] The pioneering women who first registered in various provincial associations are the subject of chapter 4. But we know even less about the hundreds of women like Ebba Nilsson who presumably obtained a considerable amount of knowledge and expertise in architecture but never practised. Their names and stories are absent from the historical record because their contributions to architecture were made entirely from outside the boundaries set by the structure of professional organizations, as noted in chapter 2.

This chapter explores how the major professional magazine in Canada, the *RAIC* [Royal Architectural Institute of Canada] *Journal*, represented women in visual images (photographs, advertisements, drawings) from 1924 to 1973.[4] Since it represented the male-dominated profession for more than five decades, the images this influential journal published acted as non-verbal statements of how the profession in Canada perceived women during a period that saw tumultuous changes in the way architecture was practised, the development of Modernism in Canadian architecture, and the slow acceptance in this country of women as registered architects. In this way, the journal acted simultaneously as a barometer of change and a tool of control for the male-dominated profession of architecture.

Following the methods of material-culture studies, in our study every minor and major reference to women in the *RAIC Journal* was copied, counted, mapped, and analysed.[5] The recurring issues associated with women members and the larger editorial and advertising patterns in the journal became immediately apparent once isolated from the general, male-centric text. The limited aims of this chapter are to show how visual images published in the journal served to reinforce the exclusivity of the architectural profession in three distinct ways. The journal, through its various representations of women, marginalized their contribution to the design process by focusing on their association with housing and interiors; advertisements in the journal identified women users with particular spaces and specific building components, emphasizing their regulation of building details rather than the overall production of buildings; finally, the journal subtly projected an image of the modern architect in Canada that was quintessentially masculine.

Women on the 'Margins'

Had Ebba Nilsson been either British or American, she might have continued her interests in building into architectural practice, rather than teach in a girls' school, since women entered the architectural profession in Canada much later than their counterparts in both these countries. But this phenomenon of the creation of seemingly complementary roles for women on the sidelines of the profession, as they entered from the 1920s forward, is the image one obtains if one looks only at the printed sources. Rather than acting in the more respected role of project designer in architecture, many Canadian women contributed to architectural projects and appeared in the *RAIC Journal* in adjunct roles, as specialized consultants to men. This apparent role parallels the special places created by and for women in the health professions, among others. The development of specialized, female-dominated health professions, for example, such as physical and occupational therapy, dietetics, and, earlier, nursing, were constructed as complementary to the more central practice of therapeutic medicine.[6]

And from the perspective of the *RAIC Journal*, the earliest women pioneers in architecture appear to have been channelled into one or two specialized areas. The next chapter demonstrates the inaccuracy of this 'official' portrayal of Canadian women architects. The comparison with women physicians, nonetheless, is instructive.

In medicine, women were encouraged to enter paediatrics, gynaecology, obstetrics, and fields in preventive medicine. Similarly, in architecture, women's expertise was seen as pertaining almost exclusively to children's and women's needs. Even the most superficial perusal of the architectural press gives the impression that the earliest Canadian women architects became special experts in the architectural subfields of housing, interiors, and, later, historic preservation. These aspects of architectural practice were and are considered less prestigious than the designs of public and commercial buildings, which tend to be larger, more high-profile, and more frequently published than housing projects. With the creation of specific 'ghettos' for women within the profession, the perceived threat that they would replace men was diminished. The ghettos ensured that women's work remained wholly dependent on that of their male colleagues.[7]

The association of women's architectural work exclusively with residential design and interiors is a complex issue, developing in large part from Victorian theories of sexual difference which claimed that, because of the smallness of their brains, women were better at arranging or finishing work started by men, than at creating projects themselves. '[A woman's] intellect is not for invention or creation, but for sweet ordering, arrangement, and decision,' claimed John Ruskin (n.d., 140–1).[8]

The sexual division of space into interior/female and exterior/male is found across cultures long before the nineteenth century. As many scholars have noted, these notions are still reinforced today, as young girls are often given dolls' houses with which to play, while boys are given toys that emphasize their control over other types of institutions, natural landscapes, and/or public spaces (Loyd 1975). These gender differences in the perception of architectural space are also clearly expressed in the Canadian women's popular press; in describing their homes, for example, men writers tend to focus on structure and mechanical systems, whereas many women writers concentrate on gardens, decoration, interior arrangements, materials, and finishes.[9]

Many of these notions were given credence in the vast literature published during the final decades of the nineteenth century for women by women, offering expert advice on the arrangement of furniture and the choice of colours in household decoration, and underlining the gendered division of interiors and exteriors. This period also saw a resurgence of middle-class domestic architecture. Known throughout the English-speaking world as the 'Queen Anne Revival,' this architectural style featured steeply pitched roofs, painted woodwork, and romantic elements such as porches and turrets; its finely crafted interiors were closely associated with Victorian women's seclusion in the home.[10]

'If there is one subject more than another in which woman's talent is required, it is domestic architecture,' asserted an author in *Saturday Night* in 1911.[11] The public perception of the relatively poor design of houses, indeed, was frequently cited as the major reason for favouring the acceptance of women architects. Women's understanding of architectural details, particularly those concerning household labour or storage, for example, was often described as far superior to that of most male architects.[12]

'The architectural house-decorator does for the inside of a house exactly what the architect does for the outside' was a typical explanation in women's advice literature of the late nineteenth century (L.M.H. 1875, 84). As early as 1876, women were employed as professional, independent interior decorators in England, with close links to feminist political struggles.[13] These 'lady decorators,' as they were called, often worked closely with architects, designing furniture and interior finishes for houses, schools, and colleges, as well as contributing to the development of innovative apartment buildings for single women. Their work was often likened to other areas of concern for which women's authority was already established, such as fashion and hair design. 'Furniture is a kind of dress, dress is a kind of furniture,' claimed Mary Eliza Haweis in *The Art of Decoration* in 1881, 'which both mirror the mind of their owner' (p. 17).

Women reformers were also active in the United States at this time. As mentioned in the introduction, in 1869 home economist Catharine Beecher published her now-famous house plan in which she suggested that a rational kitchen located in the centre of the house would professionalize women's status in the home (Beecher and Stowe 1869).[14] In the early years of this century, the education of young girls in 'domestic science' or 'home economics' witnessed this same association of women's power with the planning and decoration of houses. A typical course included instruction in sewing, cooking, and cleaning, but also a considerable amount of material on house planning, furniture arrangements, and interior finishes (Adams 1994b).

In Canada, the professionalization and feminization of interior decoration occurred later.[15] Career-guidance literature published in Canada in 1920 asserts that 'one or two firms are employing women as interior decorators with considerable success' (Massey 1920, 87). Four decades later, 40.3 per cent of those classified in the census as 'interior decorators and window dressers' were women, compared with only 2.2 per cent of architects (see table B.9). Of the six Canadian art schools listed in 1920 as offering training in interior decoration, two were within established professional schools of architecture

(Massey 1920, 89).[16] When Miss Juliana Dallaire of Moose Creek, Ontario, applied to McGill's School of Architecture in 1918, she indicated interest in studying 'landscape gardening, perspective, inside decoration and work in white and ink.' She was turned down, despite her 'ladylike' interests.[17]

'Interior decorating,' one career counsellor began, 'is a singularly appropriate career for women' (Carrière 1946, 148). The same author suggested that architecture held 'a little prejudice amongst the male members of the profession against the invasion of their sphere by women' (p. 150).[18]

In 1938 the University of Manitoba became the first Canadian university to offer a course in interior decoration, set up explicitly for women students. 'Recognizing the limited field in the profession of architecture open to women, the interior decoration course was inaugurated three years ago to provide a training in design, drawing, the history of architecture and art, and certain other professional courses in colour, decoration, and the theory of design,' claimed Milton S. Osborne, director of the School of Architecture, in 1941; in 1948 the Department of Interior Design was restructured to award Bachelor of Interior Design (BID) degrees following four years of study (previously, the diploma course in Interior Decoration lasted three years). By 1954, 218 students had graduated in the program, compared with 392 graduating in architecture.[19] Presumably, most BIDs were women.

The *RAIC Journal* very clearly reflects the pressure on women to specialize in housing and interior design. In addition to the journal's focus on the residential work of women architects, its editorial policy highlighted the work of women who were housing or interiors experts with or without professional credentials. Its biases were also evident in its omissions. There was no special mention in the journal, for example, of Esther Marjorie Hill's pioneering admission to the Alberta Association of Architects (AAA) in 1925.

Instead, the journal's editorial policy emphasized the association of women and the home. The first article by a woman architectural graduate to appear in the *RAIC Journal* was one on kitchens, by Phyllis Willson Cook, in December 1935. The article was transcribed from a radio broadcast sponsored by the Ontario Association of Architects.[20]

In keeping with the literature written by home economists, Cook's advice asserted a rational, functional approach to kitchen design; she noted how the 'scientific layout of its units' had resulted in a 'smaller and more compact kitchen.' Cook also advocated kitchens that were long and narrow.[21] The brief article was accompanied by Cook's graduation photo, presumably from the University of Toronto, from which she had graduated in 1935. It was the first photo of a woman graduate to appear in the journal; her architecture degree was noted under the image. Cook also held the distinction of being the first woman to win the annual student competition supported by the RAIC. Her winning scheme for 'An Embassy in the Capital City of a Country in the Temperate Zone' had been published in March 1934.[22] Following graduation, she worked for two years in the Interior Decorating Department of Eaton's department store in Toronto; when she died at the age of forty-two in 1954, she had designed seven houses.[23]

The *RAIC Journal* also noted women's growing role in housing reform without necessarily including their pictures. In January 1938, a notice appeared of Helen Spence's involvement in a 'Report on Housing Conditions in Toronto.' Renowned U.S. housing reformer Catherine Bauer Wurster was the first woman guest lecturer at the annual meeting of the Ontario Association of Architects, noted by the journal in March 1943 (Torre 1977, 136–8).[24] And as late as 1950, a photograph printed in the journal showed apron-clad women students learning to cook in a home-economics room. Rather than highlight the roles of women in kitchen design, however, the illustration was one in a series intended to show the work of the architects of the Toronto high school in which it was set.[25]

Similarly, women's supposed aptitude for decoration and interiors is clearly mirrored in the journal. As early as 1935 – nearly two decades before a building designed by a woman architect was featured – a photograph of the rather exotic interiors of a Toronto restaurant, Diana Sweets, appeared in the journal. A credit to interior decorator Minerva Elliot appeared under the names of the restaurant's architects, Marani, Lawson and Morris.[26] Freda G. James, a Toronto interior decorator, published a major article in the *RAIC Journal* on the use of colour, and was noted several times as the interiors consultant on public and commercial buildings in the late 1950s.[27]

Advertisements in the journal also underlined women's association with building interiors, both domestic and commercial in nature. For example, a typical advertisement for Glidden paint from 1957 (see figure 3.1) featured a nearly full-page photo of the monumental Imperial Oil office building in Toronto designed by architects Mathers and Haldenby. The text below the photo boasts that Glidden paint was used for the 'magnificent' and 'important' Canadian building. A tiny photograph included with the text shows a team of four women; an accompanying caption explains that this 'color studio' will 'help' architects to plan 'effective interior color schemes.' The not-so-subtle assumption of this and many other advertisements featuring women as interiors consultants was that women's aptitude in architecture involved only interiors, and that this kind of work was complementary, rather than fundamental, to the design process. 'This service,' the text explained to its architect-readers, 'is yours for the asking.'

3.1   Glidden advertisement. *RAIC Journal*, January 1957, 31

Even in the 1970s, advertisements in the *RAIC Journal* continued to show only female interior designers, while the clients and architects depicted were exclusively male. The manufacturers of construction systems, such as the movable partitions for office buildings made by Canadian Gypsum Ltd and promoted in the journal in 1971, emphasized the ease and flexibility of their product. One ad (figure 3.2) shows two men and a woman studying the plan of an office building. The woman, wearing a red dress and sunglasses, is an interior designer; she carries a book of material swatches under her left arm while she points to the plan with her right hand. The man seated to her left holds a pencil; another slightly behind him bites his lip in concentration. The men are making the decisions. The Ultrawall system that she is suggesting to them comprises prefabricated, lightweight panels that fit a five-foot module already established by the building architect. In addition to promoting the product, the advertisement also included the line 'It's a pleasure to design interiors,' suggesting, like other advertisements in the professional press, the fanciful and entertaining nature of interiors, relative to the more serious, businesslike character of architecture.[28]

Over its nearly fifty years of publication, the journal nearly always pictured women designers as helpers, in roles that finished or embellished work initiated by men, rather than in roles as designers of entire buildings, despite the fact that women were responsible for building design throughout this period.[29] In addition to their appearance as housing experts or as specialists in interiors, women were also noted in the journal as adept in sculpture; as collaborators with their architect-husbands; and, later, as teachers, assistant editors, and critics. Images of women as students appeared most often, however, foreshadowing the significant numbers of women graduates who would face the question of professional registration in the years following the final issue of the *RAIC Journal*.[30]

Women as Users of Space

While women appeared rather infrequently in the *RAIC Journal* in adjunct roles as housing reformers or interior designers, they appeared continually in the magazine as users of space. This is most often the case with advertisements for building components, but is also true of photographs that highlight the work of male architects, such as the image of the home-economics room in the Toronto high school mentioned above.

Patterns that recur throughout the entire run of the magazine suggest (not surprisingly, in light of women's limited appearance as designers) that, while the building itself was produced by men, women regulated the details and/or

3.2 Canadian Gypsum advertisement. *RAIC Journal*, 13 December 1971, 11

the technology in the case of domestic architecture. For example, an extraordinary number of advertisements that appeared in the *RAIC Journal* depict women or girls in bathrooms and kitchens. As the spaces in the house most often perceived as related to cleanliness and health, bathrooms and kitchens have become sites associated with both resistance to disease and the provision of food. 'As the setting for physical sustenance and hygienic care, the kitchen and bathroom – and the product worlds they frame – are crucial to intimate bodily experience,' explained Ellen Lupton and J. Abbot Miller, 'helping to form an individual's sense of cleanliness and filth, taste and distaste, pleasure and shame, as well as his or her expectations about gender and the conduct of domestic duties' (1992, 11).

Images in the journal, however, do not emphasize women's roles as medical experts or providers for their families; rather, advertisements for bathroom plumbing fixtures that appear in the Canadian architectural press show women at leisure, usually in the process of undressing. An advertisement from the Standard Sanitary Manufacturing Company that appeared in the first issue of the journal and included the company's best wishes for the magazine's inauguration, in fact, featured a woman dressed in lingerie, bending to test the temperature of her bath water. As she bows to touch the water, she gently lifts her slip to reveal her high-heeled pumps.

That same year, Fairfacts Fixtures (see figure 3.3), a U.S. manufacturer, ran an ad with a young girl disrobing in front of the bathroom sink. The girl's back is the main focus of the image, although she looks towards her image in the mirror. The details of her reflection are obscured.

This overt association of women's bodies with household technology has also been noted by museum curator Ellen Lupton (1993), who has shown how advertisements for telephones, washing machines, irons, toasters, and even typewriters, that appeared in various types of magazines included messages of romantic love and sexual gratification to prospective buyers. By including in the images only parts of women's bodies – arms, legs, backs, torsos – advertising portrayed women as mere extensions of the machines they were promoting, rather than designers or controllers of that technology.

Perhaps the best example of this notion in the *RAIC Journal* is the advertisement for Crane's 'Futura' bathroom, which appeared in May 1969. In this ad a woman's lower arm is shown installing a bathroom in a dollhouse-like construction model. A young woman, seemingly unaware that she is exposed to us, is shown undressing in the tiny bathroom. The use of the dollhouse in the image reinforces the idea that women designers' relationship to space is less serious (and more playful) than would be suggested by using a real house or an actual architectural model.[31]

3.3   Fairfacts advertisement. *RAIC Journal*, April–June 1924, ix

These relatively negative images of women in the professional architectural press are in direct contrast to those produced in the same period in women's popular magazines. *Canadian Homes and Gardens*, for example, published numerous advertisements for building materials showing couples hovering over architectural models. These images (see figure 3.4), which include women's as well as men's heads (or whole bodies) rather than focusing on women's limbs, imply that women as well as men make rational decisions regarding the design of their houses. The inclusion of the entire miniaturized model, in contrast to the dollhouse room detail, also casts women's role as more dominant and more serious than do images in the architectural press. In addition, the products advertised in these images – roofing materials, landscape features, and even household insurance – point to women's participation in exterior, as well as interior design.

This theme of women's bodies functioning as extensions of household technology is also evident in advertisements in the *RAIC Journal* for heating, ventilating, and air-conditioning equipment; the assumption here is always that women 'warm' the building.[32] 'Miss Johnson, like all human beings, is warm-blooded,' stated the advertisement for Lennox Direct Multizone System air conditioning that appeared in 1968 (see figure 3.5). 'Her thermostat is set at 98.6 degrees. She burns food. And generates heat. Lots of it,' the text explained. 'What a way to heat your building!' exclaimed the large, bold headline of the advertisement that showed a fashionable, bookish (she peeks out over her dark-rimmed glasses and holds a book) and, according to the text, unmarried woman, being cooly observed by two male colleagues (they are both removing their glasses, presumably to get a better look).

Another persistent theme featuring women in the journal's advertising were images intended to sell locks and doors. The gender assumptions made by designers of advertisements for door hardware are more ambiguous than those concerning both plumbing and heating equipment; perhaps the persistent inclusion of women was intended to symbolize women's roles as 'guardians' of the domestic threshold. Their juxtaposition with doors and door hardware could also be read as an explicit reference to women's purity and chastity; the thresholds depicted in the journal serve to contain women in spaces controlled by men.

The supposed danger in showing women 'crossing' this domestic threshold into the public world of men is well represented by the image that appeared in January 1962 (figure 3.6). A woman at the centre of the scene is seated on a white stool like those typically found in architectural drafting rooms. She is surrounded by four interior doors, shown in various stages of closure; five male construction workers stand around her. Her relationship to the product is

Insist on GYPROC WOOL

for your dream home

● Uppermost in the mind of every home-owner is year-'round comfort and peace of mind. Gyproc Wool provides both—permanently! It is fireproof and acts as a shield against fire. It is sanitary and vermin-proof. It never shrinks—always retains its original thickness. And it lasts a lifetime! Whatever may be your plans for your future home, ensure maximum comfort with this thick Insulation—made by experts. Insist on fire-protective Gyproc Wool—for cooler summers and warmer winters—always.

GYPSUM, LIME AND ALABASTINE, CANADA, LIMITED

Vancouver   Calgary   Winnipeg
Toronto-5   Montreal-2

GYPROC WOOL

THICK INSULATION

3.4   Gyproc wool. *Canadian Homes and Gardens*, September 1946, 79

What a way to heat your building!

Miss Johnson, like all human beings, is warm-blooded.

Her thermostat is set at 98.6° She burns food. And generates heat. Lots of it.

So much, in fact, that she and her co-workers overheat modern, tightly insulated buildings and cause the air conditioning to turn on. Even when it's cold outside.

Example: On a sunny, thirty-degree day, a crowded school, store or office will need cooling in one zone or another virtually all day long.

The heat output rises when people exercise, eat, get angry or excited.

Large people generate more heat than thin. Young people more than old. Men more than women. Lights, sun and machines add even more heat.

All this complicates the problem of providing total comfort to everyone, all the time, everywhere in a building.

We provide it by dividing the building into zones, giving each its individual custom-climate. We call them "micro-climates."

We can cool one zone and heat another the same instant. Or cool the same zone one instant and heat it the next.

We circulate the air continuously. Ventilate continuously. Clean the air continuously.

The system is called the Lennox Direct Multizone System (DMS) for single or multistory buildings: offices, factories, schools, apartments, clinics.

P.S. Lennox DMS cools free, when outside air falls below 57° F.

For information write: Lennox Industries (Canada) Ltd., 400 Paxman Road, Etobicoke (Toronto), Ontario.

LENNOX
AIR CONDITIONING / HEATING

• TM REG.

3.5   Lennox advertisement. *RAIC Journal*, October 1968, 12

3.6   Sargent door hardware advertisement. *RAIC Journal*, January 1962, 74–5

differentiated from theirs by her seated position and also by her clothing. She wears a fashionable suit, white hat, gloves, shoes, and pearls, while they wear the clothing and hardhats of construction workers. She holds a roll of drawings, presumably construction documents, and points to a door, seemingly advising two construction workers. The setting of the advertisement is ambiguous, although it seems to be a wood-frame house in the process of construction.

The point of the advertisement is clarified by the text. 'Function' and 'beauty' are united in Sargent's newest line of locks; like the interior designer (or architect?) who specifies them, the locks are fashionable.[33] In other words, the woman designer is valued for her innate sense of beauty and fashion, rather than for her intellect or capacity to reason.

Other building products shown in images including women imply soft and quiet qualities, such as carpets, flooring, and acoustic tiles. In these advertisements, in particular, women are often shown as models calling attention to the products, similar to the roles played by women on television game shows at this time. The assumption is, of course, that the beauty of the model will call attention to the beauty or effectiveness of the product.[34] These products, like

those specified by interior decorators, are often finishes and veneers to buildings, rather than structural aspects of the architecture. They serve to soften, or
even to mute, the unpredictable behaviour of users, perhaps like the women
who 'show' them. The women are usually dressed scantily and bear no obvious relationship to the use of the product. Men, at the same time, are shown
fully dressed, endorsing more essential, structural building parts, such as the
ad for concrete block featured in April 1969 (see figure 3.7).

Advertisements in the journal feature very few women at work; those
shown are almost exclusively nurses or secretaries, and these women are, not
surprisingly, almost always shown with plumbing, locks, or the 'muffling'
materials: acoustical tiles, flooring, and carpets. The images of nurses usually
referred to issues of safety and health; these sometimes, like the ad for Corbin
locks shown in January 1968, included smoke detectors.[35] Because nurses and
secretaries were understood (and depicted) as extremely busy people, these
advertisements also often stressed the products' ease of operation.[36]

Finally, women were depicted throughout the journal quite explicitly as sex
objects. Some advertisements, like that for Metalsmiths chairs published in
April 1969, went so far as to offer sexual gratification to male users. The ad
compared the chair's polished steel frame to a diamond engagement ring and
suggested that the chair induced a woman walking by to sit on the man's lap
and to touch his nose. Other images emphasized women's function as a scale
object or measuring stick. This sexist image of women was particularly blatant
during the late 1960s when Canadian architects (and the entire construction
industry) reluctantly faced total conversion to the metric system of measurement. An article discussing the advantages and disadvantages of the metric
system was illustrated by a photo of Britain's 'Miss Metric,' a bikini-clad
woman whose bust, waist, and hip measurements were cited in both inches
and millimetres (see figure 3.8). The image not only suggested Miss Metric
was an object to be measured and consumed, but also implied that her 'perfect' proportions were a useful standard for the construction industry.

The Manly Architect

Perhaps the most influential image affecting women published in the *RAIC
Journal* was the continuous suggestion that architects were powerful, virile,
and masculine. While women appeared as adjuncts to the profession and as
regulators or extensions of technology, men were shown, at least until 1971, as
completely controlling the design process.[37] In the journal, they were the
authoritative administrators; the designers of large-scale government, indus-
trial, commercial, and residential complexes; and the orchestrators of work

3.7   Ocean cement advertisement. *RAIC Journal*, April 1969, 2

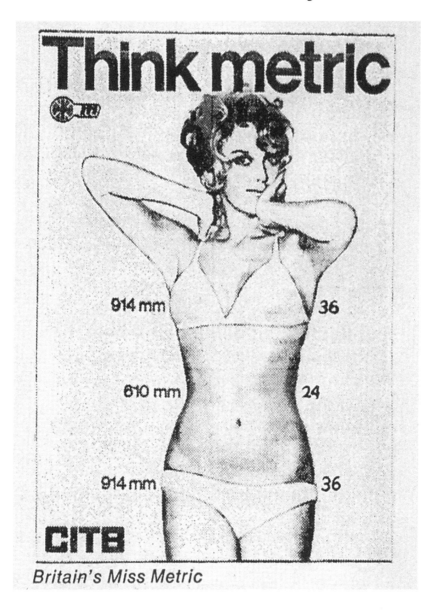

3.8   Miss Metric. *RAIC Journal*, January 1969, 57

done by others. While women in the journal appeared to be specialists, whose expertise was available 'for the asking,' men were presented as generalists, directing projects from the initial meeting with prospective clients, through design development and construction.[38]

Reinforcing this image of the architect as a secure and competent male is the frequency with which wives of male architects appeared in the journal. Many photographs of couples were shot at architectural conferences, often showing them enjoying social activities; more forceful, perhaps, was an image of a male architect at the site of an architectural project accompanied by his supportive, interested wife.[39]

Two significant articles appeared in the journal on the nature of the profession; both articles were written by women and provide evidence of the divergent views on women's roles within the profession. Catherine Chard's essay, 'What Is an Architect?' (1942), accorded no place to women in Canadian architecture. Largely a historical survey of the profession, Chard blamed nineteenth-century architects for allowing the field to degenerate into 'a weak and sentimental aestheticism.' In calling for a more collective design process, however, Chard may have assumed a more inclusive definition of the profession. In fact, this statement foreshadowed the important role played by the Montreal firm ARCOP as a place of women's employment, discussed in detail in chapter 4.

Jennifer Joynes (1959) explored women's contributions more directly than Chard in her article entitled 'Women in the Architectural Profession.'[40] Her article was the first to present statistics on the shockingly minimal progress women had made in the profession in Canada by the late 1950s. Joynes blamed the centrality of marriage in society for the scarcity of women architects; she also attempted to dispel the myths that a woman could not undertake site supervision or that her talents should be directed exclusively towards domestic projects. The article concluded with Joynes's commentary on the various accomplishments of several Canadian women architects.

Joynes's essay presented an optimistic view of the profession to readers, of whom very few were women architects. As mentioned in chapter 2, by 1960 only forty-three women in total had registered as architects in Canada (see table 2.1). In a particularly revealing section, Joynes quoted a woman architect, Anna Lam, as saying that women might appreciate the 'exterior aspect' and the 'visual and physical' effects of a new office tower in Montreal, whereas men might concentrate on the economic impact of such buildings (1959, 321). This was in marked contrast to previous associations of women with interiors only.

Joynes's assumption that the limiting factor for women's entrance into architecture was based on their personal attitudes shaped by family and social considerations is an interesting one. Her focus on the individual's failure to overcome psychological barriers minimized the constraints found within the profession, despite the fact that several references to these external barriers appeared throughout the run of the *RAIC Journal*. Two such references are particularly noteworthy, since they indicate that these problems were acknowledged by institutions within the profession: in 1941, the establishment of a diploma course in Interior Decoration at the University of Manitoba was justified as 'recognizing the limited field in the profession of architecture open to women' (Osborne 1941, 20); and, in 1964, it was reported that one of the discussions at an upcoming Congress of the International Union of Architects would involve 'the problems encountered by women architects in various countries.'[41]

Despite Joynes's optimistic and limited interpretation of the barriers that women faced in becoming architects, her article was advanced in so far as it raised, for the first time in the *RAIC Journal*, the conflicts faced by women between professional and family obligations. It was not until 1970 that these issues were mentioned again, this time in a notice for the Third International Conference of Women Engineers and Scientists, which announced that a main topic for discussion would be women's professional and family duties.[42]

The *RAIC Journal* did not ignore completely the work of Canadian women architects; the magazine was, however, extremely selective as to which women architects' work it published, and the type of project illustrated in the influential magazine. By far the women architects to receive the fullest coverage were Mary Imrie and Jean Wallbridge, Architects, of Edmonton.[43] The *RAIC Journal* covered the extensive travels of these prolific women, who designed houses, schools, and other public buildings, on their trips to eastern and western Europe, the Middle East, South America, and Asia.

Perhaps Imrie's position on the journal's editorial board from 1949 to 1960 led to the publication of at least two of the firm's projects. Despite the fact that they designed a variety of building types, the projects by the firm published in the journal were exclusively housing.[44] Imrie herself commented on the assumption made by clients that women architects might excel in domestic design. 'People will get us to do their houses, be thrilled with them and go to larger male firms for their warehouses or office buildings.'[45]

The journal's portrayal of Imrie and Wallbridge was of two fiercely independent women who travelled the globe and 'reported' on architectural and planning issues to the Canadian architectural community. They wrote five major articles for the journal on their observations of architecture and practice in other lands, from 1948 to 1958.[46] A photograph of Imrie and Wallbridge eating breakfast at a Japanese inn accompanied one of the three reports they contributed in 1958.

Readers may have been surprised that these two 'lady architects' travelled by jeep across South America and by cargo ship and camel in Asia, and dared to criticize the much-loved Modern masterpiece Chandigarh by Le Corbusier. The journal referred to the pair's travels as 'private researches.'[47] Readers may also have remarked on the women's non-traditional lifestyle; the two unmarried women lived and worked in a building of their own design known as 'Six Acres.'[48]

Another important 'type' of woman architect pictured in the *RAIC Journal* is well represented by Blanche Lemco van Ginkel, who generated a number of 'firsts' for Canadian women in architecture, and whose career is considered in depth in chapter 4. Like Imrie and Wallbridge, van Ginkel operated in a truly international context, clearly reflected by the numerous reports of her activities in the journal. And also like Wallbridge, van Ginkel's student work was published long before she began her successful design practice.[49] The journal includes publications of her design and research projects, and notices of her numerous awards and of her participation on juries.[50] What distinguishes her 'image' in the journal from that of other Canadian women architects, however, is both its academic context and the fact that it involves large-scale, urban planning projects.

Like many Canadian women architects – van Ginkel included – Freda M. O'Connor and Pamela Cluff were in partnership with their husbands. O'Connor's presence in the journal, however, is distinguished more by her pioneering role as an active administrator in the Alberta Association of Architects than as a designer.[51] In many photographs of executives, councils, and committees, O'Connor appears as the sole woman.[52] The firm's large-scale married-student housing project for the University of Alberta was published in November 1967.

Cluff's husband, A.W. Cluff, contributed to the magazine quite directly as *Architecture Canada*'s expert on the subject of architectural specifications. Pamela Cluff's publications, too, were quite technical in nature. She authored an essay titled 'Two Lift Slab Schools' that appeared in the *RAIC Journal* in 1957; it described in detail this form of concrete construction, which eliminated heavy formwork altogether. Together the Cluffs wrote a lengthy article on curtain wall construction in 1960 for *The Canadian Architect*. That magazine acknowledged their 'partnership' quite openly, noting the couple was both 'a family and a firm' and also stating the couple's two young daughters were 'co-authored' by the team.[53] Two of Pamela Cluff's projects, a swimming pool and a senior citizens' home, were included in Joynes's (1959) important essay. Cluff is an established expert on the needs of both the elderly and disabled persons.[54]

The five women 'featured' in the journal – Imrie and Wallbridge, van Ginkel, O'Connor, and Cluff – were certainly exceptional in terms of their 'visibility' in the profession. Most of the women working in architectural offices from the 1920s through the 1970s were faceless and anonymous, their contributions to the profession remaining completely invisible. There are clues in the journal, however, that they did enjoy a presence in architectural firms, albeit a small one. A telling article on five well-known architects' offices, for example, which appeared in 1948, featured interior photos of the firms' quarters as well as drawings showing the general arrangements of the offices. Of six photos of drafting rooms, five include women drafting (see figure 3.9).[55] These women were unlikely to have been registered architects at a time when 2.5 per cent or fewer architects were women, according to the census (see table B.9 for 1941 and 1951); rather, they were probably women who never obtained professional registration.[56] These women, un-registered professionals, are the focus of chapter 5.

In general, however, it seemed to be women's lack of 'manly' qualities that barred them from full acceptance to the profession in Canada, rather than any inability, lack of experience, or lack of desire to become architects. Architectural historian Andrew Saint, in his book *The Image of the Architect*, does not mention women's involvement in the profession; for him, the small numbers of women who have dared to enter the profession have had negligible influence. He stresses, indeed, how the public conception of the architect as a gentleman was central to the profession during the interwar years (Saint 1983, 96–114). The visual images published in the *RAIC Journal* imply similar biases in Canada.

Conclusion

Although women's presence in the architectural profession in Canada has been increasing steadily since the 1920s, and dramatically since 1980 (see tables B.7 and B.8), the obstacles preventing women's total acceptance, at least through 1973, continued to thrive. The *RAIC Journal* is admittedly no absolute reflection of reality; this is, in fact, the point of the next chapter. The journal was, nonetheless, a major arena through which the architectural profession in Canada developed its self-image as the century progressed.

This chapter has focused on the visual images printed in issues of the journal; its own internal administration, however, is equally powerful evidence for the

3.9   Photo of Nobbs & Val office. *RAIC Journal*, October 1948, 377

difficulties faced by women in architectural journalism. The *RAIC Journal* hired its first woman assistant editor in 1962; many of the articles which high- lighted women's contributions to architecture were found in a special section on 'Allied Arts,' edited by 'sculptor, writer and art educator' Anita Aarons.[57]

Images in the *RAIC Journal* served as real barriers to women architects in Canada. These barriers were often unwritten and unspoken. Whereas the offi- cial policy and regulations of the RAIC as an organization may have seemed relatively open to women, for example, images in the journal show clearly the kind of systematic prejudices in the schools, the profession, and the construc- tion industry in Canada throughout the period.

Ebba Nilsson retired from teaching after twenty-eight years. She died in 1988. Her photograph (and her unrealized architectural projects) were never published in the *RAIC Journal*.

4

Building the Foundations: Women Contribute to Architectural Practice

'As a friend of my mother's said when I started in at McGill [in 1942], what's your daughter want to take architecture for, that's a man's job,' recounted a woman architect who practised in Ontario in 1951–2. 'And my answer was something that came to be said more in the sixties rather than the forties, and that was "Why not?"' (F:25). This chapter explores the general contributions of some of the first women in Quebec to ask 'Why not?' vis-à-vis a career in architecture.[1] Despite the substantial barriers constructed by twentieth-century society, the professional associations, the architectural press, and the system of architectural education, these women purposefully registered as professional architects and, indeed, played leading roles in the development of Canadian Modernism.

The chapter begins by identifying patterns in the types of projects and working experiences of architects in Quebec, where women were admitted as professional architects much later than elsewhere in the country. This story is then explored against a backdrop of women from Ontario. This mode of working backwards in time underlines our intention to show how the nature of women's architectural practice in Quebec was notably distinct from that in other parts of Canada, a subject we explore in detail in chapter 6.

The larger point to be made in this chapter is that, in general, the contributions of Canadian women architects differed substantially from what the image of them presented in the professional press (as outlined in chapter 3) might suggest; as well, their experiences differed from those of their counterparts in other Western nations. Secondary literature on women in the United States and Britain has emphasized the fact that women practitioners were often marginalized by the sexist nature of architectural education and by the dominance of their male colleagues in provincial associations. As a result, British and American women have been portrayed as specialists in traditional housing, interior design, and, later, historic preservation, subfields of architecture that emphasized women's supposedly innate understanding of things domestic, as well as their 'natural' ability to preserve and/or maintain buildings rather than create new ones. Architectural historian Gwendolyn Wright has explained how, in the United States, these 'women's fields ... evolved as areas of specialization where it was permissible for women to practise, since here they were dealing with other women's needs' (1977, 280). We saw in chapter 3 how the major professional journal in Canada, *RAIC Journal*, reinforced these particular roles for women.

'Real' sources (the design projects of Canadian women architects, the personnel records of architectural firms, newspaper and journal articles, drawings, photographs, and personal interviews), however, suggest that women have contributed in significant ways to the design of many types of Canadian buildings intended to accommodate the needs of both men and women. We believe, in fact, that the diversity of Canadian women's expertise developed in spite of (or perhaps even in order to counter) the pressures exerted within architectural curricula and the press to curtail women's involvement as architects. Women architects, especially in Quebec, were thus in a position to transform the workplace, rather than be transformed by it, as other scholars, such as Wright, have suggested. In this sense, the image of women architects as projected in the journal was for the most part fictionalized; this comparison, as it were, of imaginary images and real lives underlines the grave danger of using such sources in women's history.[2]

Megastructures and Megacareers: The Quebec Case

Most of the women practising architecture in Quebec before 1970 gained their early experience in the design of high-profile, non-residential buildings. A number of major building projects in Montreal offered women architects unique opportunities, particularly Place Bonaventure and Expo 67. It is no coincidence, we believe, that the breakthrough in advertising described in chapter 3 occurred at precisely the same time.

The Royal Commission on the Status of Women, chaired by journalist Florence Bird, was also established in February 1967. Over four years, the commission met 178 times, held 37 days of public hearings, received 468 briefs and about 2,000 letters of opinion, and succeeded in no small measure in raising the awareness of average Canadians of women's position in society.

The architectural events of the late 1960s were equally pivotal. Place Bonaventure was designed by ARCOP [Architects in Cooperative Partnership] & Associates in 1962–6 (see figure 4.1). Its multiple requirements and

4.1   Place Bonaventure, Montreal. Photograph by Annmarie Adams

sophisticated connection to both railway and subway systems marked it as a 'megastructure.' This innovative design and its subsequent inclusion in Reyner Banham's book in 1976 secured Montreal's position in an international, avant-garde design movement (Banham 1976, 120–5; Viloria 1994). In 1965, five of Quebec's eighteen women architects were employed at ARCOP and were involved in one way or another with the project.

Similarly, Expo 67, the world's fair marking Canada's Centennial in 1967, provided unprecedented opportunities for Canadian women architects in large-scale planning and construction, and brought several of them international attention. The unique experiences offered at this 'brilliantly ordered visual world' may explain in part why a number of women architects in Quebec were drawn to city planning as a way of extending their architectural interests.[3] Several early Quebec women architects also worked in-house for major banks and for the federal government. Only two early Quebec women architects, in fact, truly focused on residential design.

Eva Hollo Vecsei's career was perhaps most affected by Place Bonaventure.[4] Vecsei was an associate at ARCOP in the mid-1960s, having joined the firm in

1958, and she worked intensely on Place Bonaventure under the firm's partner-in-charge, Raymond Affleck. In the substantial press coverage of Montreal's new megastructure, Vecsei's gender was called out in high relief. She clearly resented the implications. When the *Montreal Star* interviewed her in the summer of 1965, for example, she said, 'Please don't put me in the category of women who add their little pink touches ... I'm not interested in home-building projects that are uniform and repetitious ... Huge massive structures that allow for individual expression and require complex solutions to integrated problems excite me.'[5] Vecsei's apparent resistance to and awareness of such a 'category' is emblematic for Quebec women architects in the 1960s.

And Place Bonaventure catapulted her into the city's architectural foreground. The new building was one of the largest in the world at the time it was constructed, occupying a 6-acre site, including 1 million square feet of retail space, and 100,000 square feet of office area. It cost $80 million in 1967 dollars. It couldn't be further, in fact, from so-called women's architecture. It was new, expensive, massive, and multifunctional, and had enormous implications for the urban design of Montreal.

Banham pointed out both the significance of Place Bonaventure's location and its promise in his influential book:

> The point at which the two perspectives on Montreal actually meet at right-angles, where the pedestrian plumbing and the Metro intersect and the whole promise of a subterranean city protected from the elements comes closest to realization, is Place Bonaventure. Located at the first point where the Metro can comfortably squeeze under the CNR, which is also the point where the pedestrian plumbing would naturally break out to the surface, Place Bonaventure is, appropriately if disputably, a megastructure in itself. (1976, 120)

Indeed, Vecsei's work has been widely praised for its excellent use of Modern forms. When she was named an honorary fellow of the American Institute of Architects in 1990, her architectural accomplishments were praised as 'making Modernism into a language that is expressive, contextual, and symbiotic.'[6] Interestingly, she is the only Canadian woman included (among eleven Canadian men) in the 1980 directory titled *Contemporary Architects*. As also noted in the 1987 edition by editor-author Mildred Schmertz, Place Bonaventure gave Vecsei the chance to display a nearly full range of design abilities: 'her own geometric and spatial skills, her knowledge of architectural form and theory, and the power to coordinate, integrate and synthesize the knowledge of others' (1987, 946). The gestation of such skill, knowledge, and power (no 'pink touches') is crucial to this study.

4.2   Housing project by Eva Vecsei. Courtesy of Eva Vecsei

No other woman in Quebec in the immediate post-war period had the range of experiences that Vecsei brought to Place Bonaventure. Although born in Vienna in 1930, she immigrated to Canada from Hungary, where women architects were a sizeable percentage of the profession. When Vecsei arrived in Montreal in 1957, after the Hungarian revolution, she brought a portfolio of large-scale, constructed projects. She also had impressive credentials as an educator, having been an assistant professor at the School of Architecture, University of Technical Sciences, Budapest, during 1952–3. Among the architectural projects she had completed before her arrival were housing for miners in Tatabanya, Hungary, and the Lagymanyos School and Housing project in Budapest (see figure 4.2).

Other studies of professional women have presumed that the absence of men in Quebec during the Second World War provided the ultimate opportunity for women to enter the profession. This is undeniable. However, as indicated in chapter 2, our research also points to the important role played by immigrant women such as Vecsei, particularly those from Eastern Europe, in Canada following the war.[7] In fact, we believe that the case *for* women architects in the development of Modernism was very much contingent on the influx of women architects from other countries after the war. On the basis of our interviews with pre-1970 entrants, of the eighteen early Ordre des architectes du Québec (OAQ) registrants, twelve were born abroad. No fewer than seven of these hailed from Eastern Europe.[8] The cultural backgrounds of the numerous women born in countries where women architects were already a sizeable percentage of the profession by the post-war period gave them the knowledge, skill, and experience to make it in the male-dominated Montreal architectural scene, and certainly dwarfed the impact of both anglophone and francophone Canadian-born women.

'Eastern Europe (and I am told Hungary in particular) recognized women in the professions much earlier than North America. This led to a natural acceptance of these fields within the family,' commented Vecsei's contemporary Anne-Marie Balazs Pollowy, a member of the OAQ from 1964 to 1973.[9] Women who had begun their architectural education elsewhere and then immigrated to Canada were particularly aware of this difference. One such architect commented: 'I thought there was something wrong with me. I couldn't understand their attitude. Especially coming from Greece, where it was normal for women to be in architecture ... half of the students in architecture were women, even in 1946' (F:2).

Vecsei went on to design the highly controversial project La Cité, first as an associate of ARCOP's Dimakopolos, and, after 1973, under her own name. La Cité was a $120-million mixed-use urban development that opened for the 1976 Olympics; it attracted quite a bit of attention because of its potential negative impact on the surrounding neighbourhood, which was mostly row houses and small-scale development. Even urban-planning critic Jane Jacobs came to Montreal to try to protect the old neighbourhood of Victorian triplexes and apartment buildings, popularly known as the 'McGill Ghetto.' Vecsei's project included a 26-storey office building, a 500-room hotel, three residential clusters with more than 1,300 units, a shopping area of 100 boutiques, and a health club.[10] Although she attempted to break down the scale of the enormous complex with open spaces and careful massing, it nonetheless overshadowed the people-friendly neighbourhood and called for blocks and blocks of housing to be demolished.

It is important to note that the developers of La Cité – Concordia – were willing to take a chance with Vecsei – who was prepared to start her own office – because they had worked with her for nearly ten years, first on Place Bonaventure and then on the initial planning for La Cité. Admittedly, the project was a hot potato, and it is certainly telling that the first major commission to go to a Montreal woman architect working on her own was one initially rejected by her male colleagues. It is equally interesting from the perspective of women architects that, in covering the project, the press placed little emphasis on Vecsei's gender. Most of the earlier Place Bonaventure clippings, on the other hand, had stressed her perspective as a woman and her 'attractiveness.'

These three characteristics of Eva Vecsei – that she hailed from Eastern Europe, that she gained significant experience at ARCOP, and that she did not follow the traditional career path of designing kitchens and porches – are typical of the Quebec pioneers. As mentioned earlier, many of them (twelve of eighteen) were born abroad, and a significant number began and/or completed their architectural education in other countries.

Sarina Katz and Pauline Barrable are cases in point. Pauline Clarke Barrable was born in England, educated at the University of Manitoba, and first registered with the OAQ in 1969. Between 1976 and 1982, she was project architect for the Royal Bank Centre in Ottawa (see figure 4.3) for the firm of David Boulva Cleve (DBC), with whom she worked for eighteen years.[11] DBC, like ARCOP, employed a number of early Quebec women architects: Barrable, Dorice Brown Walford, and Tiuu Tammist O'Brien.[12] Far from an expert in so-called women's architecture, Barrable went on to become senior architect for the Royal Bank of Canada between 1986 and 1992.

Not surprisingly, from 1965 to 1967, she had worked as a member of Place Bonaventure's 'design/build team.' In describing the excitement of working on the project, Barrable said, 'You would literally do a drawing on the board and then pick it up off the board and run across the street ... and say "build this" and they literally would pour the concrete.'[13] This notion of a more interactive design process, whereby clients, architects, and contractors worked together simultaneously, rather than linearly, was an extremely progressive idea in the 1960s, and a key aspect of Place Bonaventure's design and construction. Parts of the building were still being designed while others were being constructed, as Barrable remembered.[14] Affleck described this process in 1966: 'I would propose that as a general theory of urban design process these events (programming, designing, scheduling, budgeting and constructing) must occur at the same time and in a situation of active dialogue' (1966, 46).

Sarina Altman Katz was born in Romania in 1934. From 1967 to 1978 she worked in the office of Moshe Safdie as Senior Project Architect on a number of the Habitat projects (New York, Puerto Rico, Israel). Not surprisingly, she had also worked at ARCOP – as a student during the summer of 1959. Katz went on to work in several other well-known offices, responsible for the design of civic squares, shopping centres, and residential projects. Her career profile clearly shows that she was responsible for all aspects of design: financial, administrative, construction, marketing, and programming.

And like many early Canadian women architects, Katz was an award-winning student. Indeed, most women architects registered before 1970

4.3   Royal Bank Centre, Ottawa. Photograph by Jill Trower

received top marks in their classes. Most significantly, their design projects and drawings were frequently published in national journals, further evidence that their work reflected current trends in design. Katz's thesis project for a music centre (see figure 4.4) was published in *Architecture–Bâtiment–Construction* in 1960. It received second prize in the national Pilkington Travelling Scholarship and Award the same year and was described by the jury in thoroughly Modern terms: 'the forms lent themselves admirably to their function – a thoroughly organic and well-integrated plan solution.'[15]

Another pioneering Modernist who gained valuable experience at Expo 67 was Blanche Lemco van Ginkel. As mentioned in chapter 3, she established a number of firsts for women in architecture in this country, in both academic and professional settings. In terms of the RAIC alone, she was the first elected officer in 1972, and first elected fellow in 1973. Her appointment as Dean of Architecture at the University of Toronto in 1977 represented a first for North America.[16] And she has actively promoted an appreciation for the work of Canadian women architects through her publications.

As a principal of Van Ginkel Associates, Blanche van Ginkel participated in a study of the circulation patterns of downtown Montreal (see figure 4.5), the original master planning of Expo 67 (see figure 4.6), and other very public projects. Like Vecsei, van Ginkel married an architect and practised with him. Seven (more than one-third) of our eighteen case-study women in Quebec married architects; another four married men in related fields (engineers, contractors). In many of our interviews, women mentioned the significance of their supportive husbands, who were well aware of the difficulties involved in architectural practice.

Many women architects met their husbands while at school, and typically the young couple secured employment at a single firm, eventually setting up a practice together. Eva and André Vecsei met at the University of Budapest, married in 1952, and worked together at ARCOP from 1958 to 1962. They went into practice as Vecsei Architects in 1984. Vecsei stresses the importance of having a supportive husband: 'André is very masculine. He would never do the kitchen things. But he was really good about the broad and basic things, like the children. And he wanted me to continue working. At times, it was really tough for me.'[17]

Few Canadian women architects, relative to their U.S. counterparts, feel their work is overshadowed by the achievements of more-famous husbands. Again the example of Denise Scott Brown (married to Robert Venturi) is relevant, as she has spoken out on many occasions on what she calls the 'star system.' Although she and her husband co-authored the now-classic *Learning from Las Vegas*, Venturi receives all the credit: 'As a wife, I am very happy to

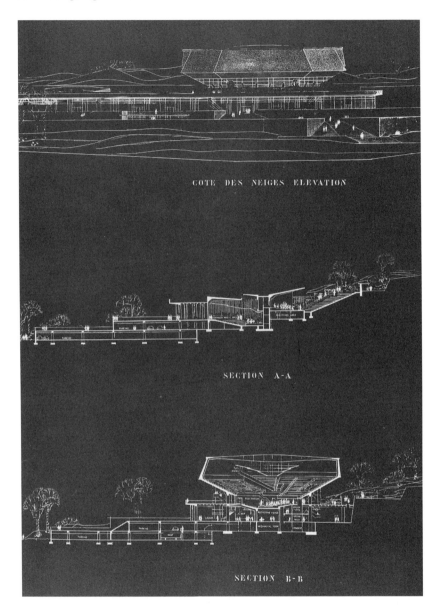

COTE DES NEIGES ELEVATION

SECTION A-A

SECTION B-B

4.4 Sarina Altman Katz's thesis project for a music centre in Montreal, published in *Architecture-Bâtiment-Construction*, July 1960, 37. Collection Centre Canadien d'Architecture/Canadian Centre for Architecture, Montreal

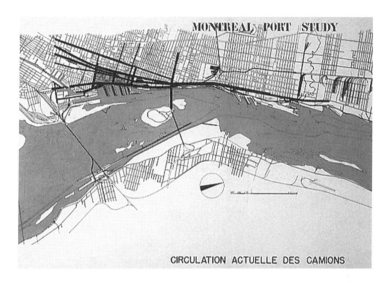

4.5 Plan of Old Montreal from Blanche Lemco van Ginkel's study. Blackader-Lauterman Library, McGill University

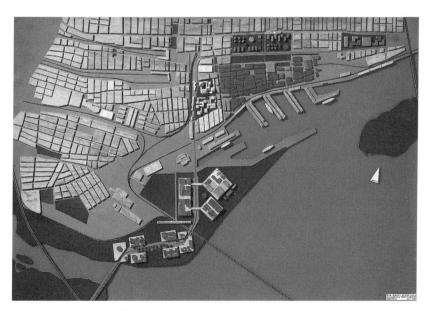

4.6 Presentation model of Expo 67. Collection Centre Canadien d'Architecture/Canadian Centre for Architecture, Montreal

see my husband honored, but as a collaborator I feel very unhappy to see my work attributed to Bob ... We have developed a body of theory together that owes a great deal to both of us. It is difficult to unseam it' (Greer 1982, 48).[18]

In quite a few cases, the parents or parents-in-law of our interviewees had been architects, which could have been a source of bitterness, according to Scott Brown's 'star system.' It also helped them, however, to secure employment. Following her graduation from the Massachusetts Institute of Technology in 1940, Helen Bunker married architect John Kenneth Ross, son of George A. Ross, a partner in the well-known architectural firm Ross and Macdonald. This firm is one of the most important in Canadian architectural history, responsible for the design of Toronto's Union Station and Royal York Hotel, the Mount Royal Hotel in Montreal, the Château Laurier in Ottawa, and a number of stores for Eaton's. Helen Bunker Ross worked for 'two stretches of about a year each for Ross Peterson Townsend & Fish,' registering in 1946 (resigning in 1954).

While marriage to architects (or sons of architects) in most cases helped women to secure employment, it also ensured, at least in the post-war period, that women were paid less. 'They couldn't see why we needed two salaries,' remembered one interviewee about working in the same office as her architect-husband (F:2). Marriage to other architects also affected women's timing vis-à-vis registration. Henriette Barrot Chenevert, for example, worked with her architect-husband, Raoul Chenevert, for many years before even bothering to register, which she did in 1952, following his death.[19]

A similar example from outside Quebec is that of Ilsa Julia Clara Williams, an Australian-born architect who practised with her husband, William Frederick Williams, in Nelson, B.C., from 1935 until her retirement in 1957. It was only after his death in 1947 that her name became associated with the firm's designs, which included housing, hospitals, schools, and government buildings.[20]

Van Ginkel's interest in city planning, as she pointed out to us, may have been inspired by her position as one of few women in a male-dominated profession. As we discuss in chapter 5, it was also a common way that women architects extended architectural practice:

> In the mid-'40s and '50s, when town planning was beginning to emerge as an enterprise in Canada, several women found employment more readily in that field than in architecture – Catherine Chard and I being two of them. This may have been because we were offered jobs by Eugenio Faludi whose background was European. But I also think that it was because it was a 'new' profession in Canada, without the old traditions of the architecture profession.[21]

Indeed, city planning attracted several early women architects in Quebec, including Chard and Evanthia Zoumboulidou Caragianis. With its broad mandate and concerns such as transportation, large-scale pedestrian circulation, and site usage, planning could not have been further from the traditionally 'feminine' side of architecture, especially interior design. Van Ginkel explains, 'It is unlikely that [city planning] was perceived to relate to "feminine" qualities and domestic experience (like interior design). I went into planning as an extension of architecture, but other women entered the field without a background in architecture.' Perhaps their experiences at Expo 67 also attracted these young women to planning.

There is anecdotal evidence to suggest, however, that the trend was international. In the United States, for example, several well-known women architects were also drawn to planning. Particularly interesting in light of the Canadian situation are those whose husbands were notable practising architects: Catherine Bauer Wurster and Denise Scott Brown. British architect Allison Smithson is another case in point. This tendency to combine their architectural expertise with planning perhaps also reflects what architectural historian/critic Dolores Hayden (1984) suggests is the notion of community nurturing the efforts of U.S. women architects. As she has pointed out, this often led to neighbourhood or city planning. Many women architects served on community boards as well, particularly those of schools, churches, and hospitals. Our interviews pointed to these contributions as significant ways in which women architects demonstrated their planning expertise. 'I feel that [serving on boards] did in some small way contribute to the recognition of female architects in the early days,' remarked Walford, looking back on her career.[22]

There is some evidence, too, that city planning offered more stability to architecture graduates than employment in strictly architectural firms, even during the construction boom following the end of the Second World War. Several women architects described their fears about financial stability, particularly those married to other architects. 'It had a lot more stability ... even when I went on my own with the planning I had contracts with the towns for at least a year. I knew that that year I was going to earn enough to manage family expenses,' remembered a graduate of the 1950s (F:2). A career in planning also provided more opportunities to work directly with people, which several women saw as more appealing than working independently in an office. '[P]lanning suited my temperament a lot more ... I dealt a lot more with people ... I was very happy with that,' recalled the same woman.[23]

Dorice Constance Brown Walford gained important early experience at Barott, Marshall, Merrett and Barott, before transferring to David, Barott,

4.7   Telephone Building, Expo 67. School of Architecture, McGill University

Boulva, which under its early 1960s title of Marshall & Merrett was the third Montreal office to employ significant numbers of women in the pre-1970 era.[24] She was born in Moose Jaw, Saskatchewan, in 1924, and attended the University of Manitoba and McGill for her M. Arch. Although she did not work on Place Bonaventure, she was also involved with Expo; she was the project architect for the Telephone Building (see figure 4.7) at the office of David, Barott, Boulva.[25]

Walford was one of the earliest women architects in Canada to specialize in an institutional building type. Far from the expected focus on houses and preservation, however, she was an expert designer of university laboratories and medical buildings; for the Montreal Children's Hospital, she did hospital design, master planning, programs determining the list of requirements, government reports, strategic planning, and studies on potential hospital mergers.[26] On McGill University's McIntyre Medical Sciences Centre, Walford was project architect at Marshall & Merrett (see figure 4.8). She was the library and space planner of the stark, Modern addition to the Allan Memorial Institute next to Royal Victoria Hospital in Montreal (see figure 4.9). Walford thus worked at

4.8   McIntyre Building, McGill University. Photograph by Annmarie Adams

4.9   Allan Memorial Institute addition, Montreal. Photograph by Annmarie Adams

two of three of the Montreal offices that tended to hire women. And although she was never employed at ARCOP, she became good friends with Ray Affleck and worked with him on several committees.[27]

Previous research on women architects has suggested that the relatively low number of women architects in Canada may have precluded any system of networking among the pioneers. Our research, however, shows that these three offices – ARCOP, DBC, and BMMB – particularly ARCOP under Affleck, served as important places of support for women in Quebec, especially Montreal. 'They were one of the few firms in the city that hired women,' remembered one early woman architect about BMMB in the 1950s. 'I was advised to go to that firm because it was known that they hired women' (F:1). Few women remember, however, *how* they came to know about these firms' reputations. 'It was just common knowledge, the students were probably talking,' was a typical response (F:1). Perhaps more important was the fact that the acceptance of women in these firms was seen inside and outside the office as particularly progressive. 'Maybe we thought we were avant-garde or some damn thing ... and they were competent,' recalls Art Nichol of ARCOP today. 'I like to think that we were pioneers.'[28]

Prior to her tenure at Marshall & Merrett, Walford had worked in Europe, first in the office of Le Corbusier, and then in the Department of Foreign Buildings Operations in Paris, where she had worked with Edward Stone, Skidmore Owings and Merrill, and Ralph Rapson. Van Ginkel's early experiences were nearly identical, although she was born outside Canada, in England (1923). In 1948, between her graduations from McGill in 1945 and Harvard in 1950, she worked at the Atelier Le Corbusier in Paris.[29] In the office of this Modern master, she was responsible for both the form of the ventilator and the decoration of the Provençal tiles on the nursery of the Unité d'Habitation. By going abroad, Walford and van Ginkel had gained invaluable experience with internationally renowned Modernists. Such experience was unavailable in Canada, perhaps even in North America, at that time. In some ways, this put their experience on a par with that of immigrant women from Eastern Europe, such as Vecsei, who had arrived in Canada as accomplished architects.

Walford and van Ginkel also shared an interest in their profession by contributing to the governance of the Royal Architectural Institute of Canada (RAIC). Walford was the first woman officer of the College of Fellows in 1987, serving as registrar for three years.[30]

At Marshall & Merrett, Walford became friends with Janet Leys Shaw Mactavish, who had graduated from McGill in 1947 (she died in 1972).[31] Mactavish was a widely respected authority on the architecture of schools and designed many of the Lakeshore schools on the west island of Montreal, such as Valois Park, Beaconsfield, and Lakeside Heights (see figure 4.10).

Like many women architects, there is scant information on her career; however, as Mactavish developed an innovative cost-evaluation method in the design of schools, her ideas were published during her lifetime, and her name is closely associated with the buildings she designed.[32] Mactavish's schools are U- and L-shaped structures that illustrate the rational, economical planning ideas popular in the 1950s. Her major idea to decrease costs was to reduce the amount of space given over to circulation. In 1956, she designed a circular school with an auditorium at its centre to illustrate this idea (see figure 4.11). Walford worked on several of these schools with Mactavish, and 'so learned a great deal with her.'[33]

Modern architecture provided women architects in Quebec with an unprecedented opportunity to contribute their expertise to the planning and design of enormous public and commercial ventures. The sheer scale of the commissions, such as Expo 67, and the speed with which projects were designed and then constructed, and new ways of working in teams (such as Place Bonaventure), and the use of new building technologies provided Quebec women architects with the experience, and perhaps the confidence, to occupy the cen-

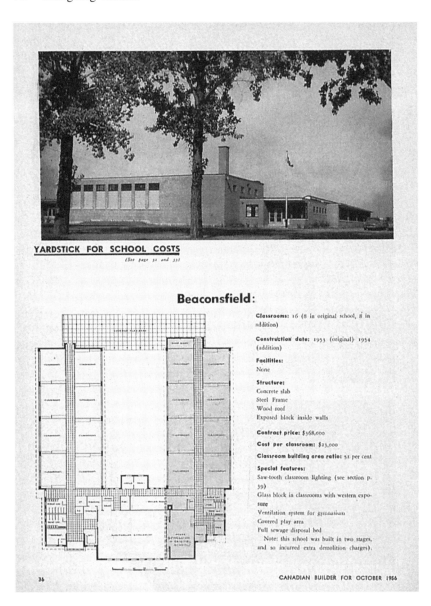

4.10   Beaconsfield School. *Canadian Builder*, October 1956, 36. National Library of Canada

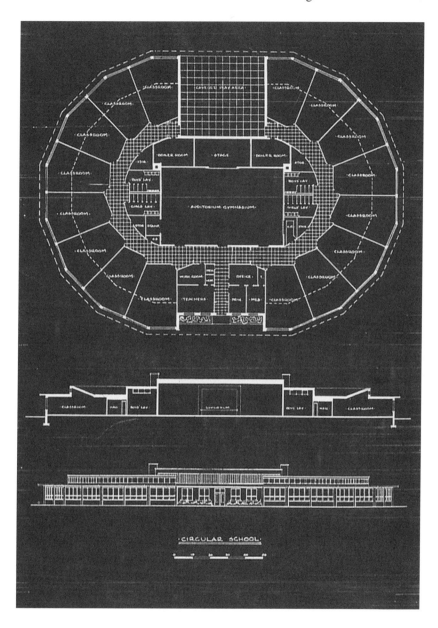

4.11   Design for a circular school. *Canadian Builder*, October 1956, 39

tre, rather than the 'margins,' of the profession. It also changed the atmosphere in the province's architectural schools such that more and more women were accepted as students.

At McGill University, in fact, the last Canadian program to include women, Modernism marked the first acceptance of a woman student: Catherine Chard Wisnicki.[34] Women were finally admitted to McGill's School of Architecture not on the basis of their own strengths, but out of the administration's growing concern about the shrinking number of students in the school. At one point, there was even a possibility that the school might close. John Bland, who was director of the school from 1941 to 1972, is frequently credited with making the necessary social and physical changes under the acting directorship of Philip Turner during 1939–41, changes that eased women's acceptance to the school. In any case, Chard Wisnicki was accepted to the program in 1939, having applied for four consecutive years. Six months later, a second woman, Arlene Ruel Scott, was also admitted.

In her early years of practice, Chard Wisnicki worked with A.J.C. Paine and with the Montreal firm of Lawson & Betts on the federal post office in St John's, Newfoundland. She also participated in the planning of Arvida, Quebec, for the Aluminum Company of Canada. Immediately following the war, she was employed by the Canadian Wooden Aircraft Company in Toronto to undertake a study of prefabricated housing. In fact, Chard Wisnicki became something of a 'prefab' expert. She was interviewed on the radio about the subject in 1944 and co-authored (with city planner E.G. Faludi) an important article on prefab housing as early as 1945.

That same year, Chard Wisnicki registered with the Ontario Association of Architects, becoming their fourth woman member. Most of her career, however, was spent with the well-known Vancouver firm Sharp, Thompson, Berwick & Pratt. There she worked closely with Ned Pratt, participating in the design of the Brooks, Saba, Gregg, and Mathers residences, all considered icons of Canadian Modernism. Later, with McGill alumnus John Porter, she designed the Daniels and Nemetz houses. 'I was one of a group of young McGill architects who settled in Vancouver and had quite an impact on the local design scene,' she recalls, modestly understating her true contribution.[35]

Others have seen her as more of a revolutionary. University of British Columbia art historian Rhodri Windsor Liscombe, for example, credits Chard Wisnicki, Porter, and McGill alumni Duncan McNab, Michael Utley, Arthur Erickson, and H. Peter Oberlander, with conveying Modernist ideals to the West Coast from Montreal (1985, 65). Architectural historian Sherry McKay, whose 1989 article on B.C. Modernism has become the classic statement on the regional style, described Chard Wisnicki's role as 'an inspiring presence.'

'The clarity of architectural ideas found in her work is often breathtaking,' adds McKay.[36]

In what now seems like an incredible coincidence, one of Chard Wisnicki's student projects, for the Boston Architects' Club, was published next to one by Blanche van Ginkel for a dancer's studio in 1942 (see figure 4.12). Of course, Chard and van Ginkel knew each other as students at McGill, sharing interests in Modern architecture and city planning, and both became successful academics. In fact, van Ginkel remembers Chard Wisnicki as a personal role model. 'My classmates – male and female alike – benefited from her frequent exhortations to examine issues in architecture with a fresh eye, to renounce dogma and to develop ideas that might serve the mid-twentieth century.'[37]

In 1963, Chard Wisnicki began teaching part-time at the School of Architecture at UBC, joining the faculty full-time a few years later. Architecture schools, like architectural firms, had very few women at that time. In fact, only 1.2 per cent of registered architects in Canada in 1961 were women (see table B.8 in Appendix B). Chard Wisnicki's innovative teaching methods, especially her passionate interest in urban issues, were an inspiration to many young women studying architecture. McKay, who currently teaches at UBC's School of Architecture, describes this special role played by Chard Wisnicki as a faculty member, noting that 'countless women were inspired by her example.'[38] Chard Wisnicki was the second woman registered with the Architectural Institute of British Columbia in 1946.

Remarkably few francophone women architects registered in Quebec in the pre-1970 period; however, the province's first woman to register was Pauline Roy Rouillard, in October 1942. Following her graduation from the École des Beaux Arts[39] in Montreal in 1941, she worked for Anglo-Shipbuilding on the construction of warships.[40] From 1943 to 1960, she worked for a number of architectural firms; from 1961 to 1968, she was in private practice. Rouillard was the senior architect for the Société d'Habitation.[41]

There is little information on the reaction to Rouillard's acceptance to the Province of Quebec Architectural Association, now the OAQ. A letter from the secretary of the association informing the young architect of her acceptance is the only extant reference to the event: 'At the meeting of Oct 2nd, members of Council expressed themselves very enthusiastic and very much concerned about your being the first lady architect admitted to exercise the profession in the province of Quebec ...'[42] A brief notice of her acceptance was noted in the RAIC Journal the same year, 'welcom[ing] this innovation.'[43]

The history of women architects in Quebec is both remarkable and paradoxical on many levels. It was dominated, in its first three decades, by women who had come to Quebec from other places; Canadian-born women were very

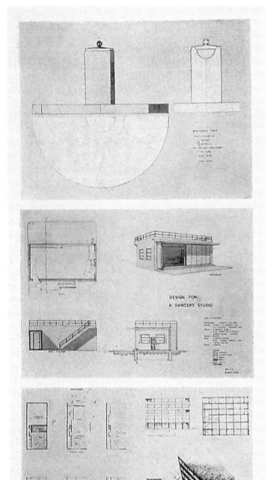

SCHOOL OF ARCHITECTURE
McGILL UNIVERSITY

FIRST YEAR
BAPTISMAL FONT
Brian O'Leary

The Baptismal font is essentially a basin for containing water raised to table height. It is a fixture of great importance in a church. It has monumental quality. Granite was the material chosen. It has a lid to keep it clean which must be easily removed; this is made of ebony. The handle represents the Cross. The font is raised upon a step so that the ceremony is elevated. This is a first exercise in searching for suitable form.

SECOND YEAR
A DANCER'S STUDIO
Blanche Lemco

The problem is to design a space of a given size to be suitable for an artist of the author's choice. The dancer has been chosen. The dancer is an athlete. He needs a perfect floor, music, fresh air, a place to rest. A roof deck is suggested. One side of the studio opens on to a terrace. This is not sentimental architecture. The building satisfies its essential purpose as it has been analysed. This is basic. What do you think, Mr. Joos?

THIRD YEAR
AN ARCHITECTS' CLUB
Catherine Chard

Boston Architects' Club, a joint problem with the School of Architecture, Massachusetts Institute of Technology, 1940-41.

The Club is a meeting place for architects, draughtsmen and workers in the allied arts. It has a social and an educational purpose. The building is to contain a great hall for meetings and exhibitions, a committee room, a lounge and restaurant, a library, class rooms and a drawing studio.

The site is open on three sides, two principal streets and a lane. The accommodation requirements and the nature of the site suggest a vertical arrangement.

The social spaces are planned upon the lower floors. The educational accommodation is on the top. The library is the link. A great stair communicates through the social floors. A service element is carried throughout the building along the inside wall from front to back. All spaces in the club would be quietly and efficiently served. The plan is neat, the structure is simple. Architectural emphasis is upon disciplined form and colour.

4.12 Student work from McGill University. *RAIC Journal*, February 1942, 26 much a minority. While many women architects in other places who had entered the profession decades earlier were forced into careers in residential design and interiors, the first women in Quebec worked on 'the big ones' and made their names in the design of huge multi-use blocks, hospitals, banks, and entire sections of cities.

This seemingly progressive situation for women at first glance seems incongruous in the province slowest to accept women as architectural students and as registered architects. We believe that it is precisely because women were admitted so late – at a time when 'megaprojects' and 'Modernism' were everyday words in the Quebec architecture milieu – that so many were able to choose career paths open to so few women in other provinces. Modernism was, of course, not exclusive to Quebec architecture, but was developed in urban centres across the country simultaneously. We believe, however, that it was this coincidence of women's entry into the profession and commissions such as Expo and Place Bonaventure that ensured Modernism would have more of an impact on women architects in Quebec than elsewhere. In Toronto and Vancouver, too, women architects participated in the Modernist project. In Quebec, however, it was the first generation who hailed its arrival. As we discuss further in chapter 6, the decades that saw the admission of women to the OAQ were a time of great social upheaval in Quebec, the so-called Quiet Revolution. And, of course, the coincidence of women's entry to the male-dominated profession of architecture with both the post-war economic boom and the development of Modernism was fortunate, to say the least.

Ontario Women Architects

The work experience of Esther Marjorie Hill, for example, Canada's first registered woman architect and the first woman graduate in architecture from a university in Canada, is much more typical of early women architects in other countries and lies in sharp contrast to the careers of Quebec architects.[44] While they designed world's fairs and megastructures, she wrote about domestic affairs for newspapers, and designed gloves. While they moved from a concentration in architecture to the broader scale of city planning, Hill used her architectural education towards the design of greeting cards and worked as an interiors consultant at a department store. While Quebec women benefited from the albeit small network of women working in three offices in Montreal, Hill was utterly alone in the profession. As has already been mentioned, the Alberta Association of Architects even changed its entrance requirements in order to keep her out.[45]

Despite the fact that Hill encountered such resistance in Ontario, it had the highest number of new women registrants – thirty – in the pre-1970 period (see table B.7).[46] It is highly likely, of course, that women in Quebec may have encountered the same degree of opposition had they even been considered as members in the 1920s.

Hill, however, was not the only one to encounter such resistance in Ontario. The first woman to register with the Ontario Association of Architects (OAA), Alexandra Biriukova, is perhaps the best known, probably because of her famous client, the artist Lawren Harris. Any fame she does enjoy today is certainly not due to present-day architectural historians, who have tried to diminish the role she played in the design of Harris's well-known house.[47] Indeed, Biriukova's exquisite design for Harris's 1930 Forest Hill home is considered by many to be an icon of Canadian Modernism, 'one of the few identifiably modern houses built in Toronto at this time' (Dendy and Kilbourn 1986, 245). During its construction, the house was featured in *Canadian Homes and Gardens*, in which it was called 'an essentially modern design, depending on its simple statement of mass, proportion, and the quality of the materials themselves for its beauty and effect.'[48] Unfortunately for the course of Canadian architecture, she resigned from the OAA in 1934 and spent the rest of her career as a tuberculosis nurse at the Free Toronto Hospital for the Consumptive Poor (Contreras, Ferrara, and Karpinski 1993; Simmins 1989, 110; van Ginkel 1991, 9).

Like many women architects a decade later, Biriukova had arrived in Canada as an architect. Born in Russia in 1895, she received her architecture degree from the School of Architecture in Petrograd. Exiled in 1914, she subsequently went to Italy, where she graduated in 1925 from the Royal Superior School of Architecture in Rome. She worked for architect Aznaldo Foshini in Rome from 1924 to 1929.[49]

So, while we can find isolated examples of women, such as Biriukova, furthering the Modernist mandate, Ontario's first women architects were much more likely to take up careers in public service, historic preservation, or housing design. These broad patterns of career choice among Ontario women architects are not limited to the era of Hill and Biriukova (in the 1920s and 1930s), but rather are most evident in the 1960s and continue to the present day.

Architectural careers in public office, of course, offered women architects many benefits rarely available in private practice. First, government jobs, especially just after the Second World War, offered much more stability than did the unpredictable cycles of private commissions. Public-service architects could predict their hours with some certainty and could count on a regular paycheque, while most architects in private practice frequently worked eve-

4.13   House designed by Barbara Humphreys, Manotick, Ontario. *Habitat*, July–August 1959, 6. National Library of Canada

nings and weekends in the period leading up to a deadline. Firms often let their junior staff go, too, immediately following the close of a project. The predictability of a career in public service was thus particularly appealing to women, who were largely responsible for arranging child care within their families. The fact that such security does not seem to have convinced Quebec women to change their career plans will be touched on in chapter 6.

Barbara Humphreys and Christina Perks, who joined the OAA in 1945 and 1969, respectively, worked as public-service architects for most of their careers.[50] Humphreys, in fact, is the 'quintessential' Ontario woman architect, specializing at one time or another in public service, historic preservation, and housing, the three areas identified as specialties particularly suited to women in the context of other countries. She graduated from the University of Manitoba in 1941, receiving first mention in the competition for the Royal Architectural Institute of Canada Award and the University Gold Medal. Her 'public' life began immediately following graduation; she found employment in the Defence Industries Limited Architectural Division in Montreal and in the Plant Engineering Division of Victory Aircraft Limited in Malton; from 1954 she worked in private practice in architecture, and was mostly occupied with the design and supervision of houses in Ottawa, Manotick, and Kingston (see figure 4.13).

Humphreys returned to public life in 1966, working as a consultant to the National Historic Sites Service. Three years later she directed a survey of the architectural heritage of the Rideau Corridor. This survey acted as a pilot project for the Canadian Inventory of Historic Building (CIHB), of which Humphreys was a founder and later chief. She retired in 1981.[51]

Christina Poznanska Perks held a number of senior positions with the Canadian government after graduating from McGill University in 1957 and is perhaps the best example of this 'manager' type of architect. She was the director of Facilities Development for External Affairs and a senior policy adviser and senior project manager at Public Works Canada in 1966–70. This background in public service may have inspired the nationalist fervour of her firm's official mandate: 'To be Canadian is to experience diverse geographic regions and the diverse cultural background of their people. To be an architect is to interpret the needs of the region and the needs of its people in built form. To be Canadian and an architect is to utilize to advantage this geographic and cultural experience.'[52]

Some Ontario women architects followed the Quebec model, although they were not typical. The best case is perhaps Marilyn Robertson Lemieux (see Gillett 1981, 322). Following her graduation from McGill in 1948, she worked on a variety of structures: naval architecture, measured drawings of hospitals, a master plan for Halifax, a company town. She even practised in Ghana from 1959 to 1961. She took about twelve years off work, 'rocking the cradle.' Following this period at home, Lemieux found the return to practice 'very frightening.' She recounts it this way:

> I had been subscribing to the architectural periodicals, but I just felt that I had forgotten all I ever knew about architecture. I even tried to think of something I might do instead as I thought too much would be expected of me in architecture ... I called Ray Affleck, who was at McGill when I was, and told him that I wanted to get on with my profession and that I had such misgivings about my ability. That apparently didn't bother him, and he invited me to go and work in his office. It turned out to be like riding a bicycle – I hadn't forgotten anything; I simply hadn't made any progress. As time went on, I improved my skills ...[53]

The career of Isobel Grace Stewart is far more 'typical' of Ontario women architects for two important reasons: her practice focused on residential design and historic preservation. These are the two most obvious patterns that emerged from our collection of material from pre-1970 women architects in Ontario: that Ontario women are more *likely* to specialize in these subfields. And, as was true of Lemieux and so many other women architects, both Stewart's education and her professional life were interrupted by family responsibilities. She began architecture school at the University of Toronto in 1938; in 1940, she married John Young, who died during the war. Her son was born in 1943, and Stewart returned to her architectural studies, graduating in 1946.

Stewart did not register with the OAA, however, until more than twenty years later, in 1967, despite the fact that she was working throughout that time period in architects' and planners' offices. The same year she opened her own office in Oakville, Ontario, concentrating on residential work. An article in the *Globe and Mail* from 1962 described many of her views on current and future housing, which tended to be extremely conservative.[54]

As in other countries, Canada's women architects have been the pioneers of the historic preservation movement, recognizing the value of recycling old structures. Humphreys, as already mentioned, was a founding member of the CIHB; Alice Ayer Alison was one of twenty founders of the Association for Preservation Technology (APT) in 1978;[55] Catherine Currie Smale was a board member of both the Ontario Heritage Foundation and the Heritage Canada Foundation. They have all been directly involved in the recycling of old buildings, in addition to these administrative accomplishments.

Although the situation is slowly changing, there is far less prestige associated with historic preservation than with new design. Entirely new construction is perhaps unfairly considered more 'creative,' since the architect is presumably designing a building for a site that was formerly empty. The care and maintenance of historic structures, of course, requires a certain amount of self-effacement on the part of a designer. Lily Inglis explains:

> It's no good thinking that you can decide every detail for everybody and that it should stay there for the rest of time. That's an arrogant view. I think that buildings should be able to cope with some change. Some people get their kicks from dreaming things up. But my kicks really come from seeing it there and even more from seeing it used and seeing people enjoying it ... In order to work with older buildings you have to pay respects to the past and to past architects, and that is a sort of humble attitude that a lot of architects aren't really interested in. They want to build their own monuments and not necessarily pay respect to the past. (Mangiacasale 1985, 8)

Joan Burt's practice in Toronto has concentrated on the renovation of historic row houses. In terms of this study, Burt's description of this niche in the competitive world of architecture as directly related to her gender was of considerable interest. 'I'm a lady in architecture. When I graduated, the bank board wasn't going to hire me. So I had to create a little area of my own,' she said (Simmins 1982/3, 148). This 'little area' of historic preservation has been a booming business in Canada since the 1960s and 1970s, coinciding directly with the jump in the numbers of women graduating from architectural programs.

The history of the historic-preservation movement in Canada has yet to be written; as in the United States, however, women (architects and others) were instrumental in building its foundations. As Barbara Howe (1992) has explained in her work on U.S. women preservationists, women's influential role in this area is linked to the movement's roots in volunteerism and community work, long the stronghold of middle- and upper-class women. In the United States, the preservation of Mount Vernon by Ann Pamela Cunningham is usually cited as the first stirrings of the preservation movement.

An equally 'humbling' subfield of the profession has been the architectural resolution of social problems, which has attracted a number of women architects from Ontario. Within that broad field, housing for the elderly has been the focus of Pamela Cluff, Gail Lamb, and Joan Grierson. Following her graduation from the University of Essex in 1952, Cluff established her practice in Toronto in 1957. Since the early 1970s, however, she has specialized almost exclusively in the design and redesign of institutions for the elderly and handicapped. This sort of work entails an enormous commitment to the community; Cluff has served on the Ontario Welfare Council, various committees in the Ministry of Housing sponsoring barrier-free design, the Ontario Fire Commission, and Mayor Crombie's committee to look at accessibility in Toronto's buildings.[56]

Housing for the elderly also comprises a large part of the practice of London-based Gail Lamb. Although a sole practitioner for thirty years, Lamb has noted how a brief association with a male partner made an enormous difference in attracting larger commissions. 'By the client's admission, I would not have been awarded a large project recently completed, without a man at my side,' she recounted.[57]

Joan Burt made precisely the same comment nearly twenty years earlier. In 1973, she was 'convinced that having an architect as a husband helps a lot when the client happens to be a large board of directors ... [They] seem to find it difficult psychologically to cope with women architects ... They like to do business in club surroundings which doesn't seem feasible when the architect is a woman,' she commented in an interview with the *Globe and Mail*. 'I'm not sure I would get jobs if clients didn't know I had a male back-up,' concurs Helga Plumb, a principal in the firm of Dubois Plumb Architects in Toronto. Plumb has won numerous awards, including the prestigious Governor General's Medal for Architecture, and her work has been featured in several books about energy-efficient design.[58] Such remarks lie in complete contrast to the comments made by Quebec's women architects of the same period, many of whom seem to resent any suggestion that they obtained commissions through male contacts.

Many Ontario women architects also remarked on the intimidation they faced at being the 'only' woman, in school, in the office, and in the professional association. Joanna Barclay de Tolly Ozdowski found it difficult to enjoy 'cigar-smoke meetings of the prominent architects' at the OAA, for example, after becoming a member in 1957.[59] Despite the barriers, however, many Ontario women architects persevered and succeeded. Ozdowski, like so many of her female colleagues, won design awards, specifically the Canadian Housing Design Award from the Canada Mortgage and Housing Corporation in 1964.

Conclusion

In Quebec, particularly in Montreal, the first registered women architects tended to work on large-scale commercial and public projects, and they were drawn to three key firms, perhaps practising an early form of feminist networking. An extraordinary number of them were qualified in and practised city planning in addition to architecture. In Ontario, on the other hand, more women (although not all of them) in the pre-1970 period focused on public service, historic preservation, and the architectural resolution of social problems.

Women architects inside and outside Quebec were clearly affected by the time period in which they entered the profession; the first women architects in Ontario, for example, registered just before and during the Great Depression, when construction all over North America came to a halt. Their counterparts in Quebec, on the other hand, who first entered architectural programs during the Second World War, faced a world desperate for new buildings upon graduation. The 1960s and 1970s in particular was the time of several megaprojects in Montreal – Expo 67 and, later, the Olympic games – offering men and women architects unmatched opportunities in design.

While Quebec was the last province to accept women as registered architects, the experiences of its 'pioneers' were much more transformatory. Even though the Ontario Association of Architects continued to accept women members during this same period, the 1960s and 1970s, they seem to have been channelled to specialize in more traditional 'women's work,' especially public service and historic preservation. Ontario women, too, tended to work more independently than women in Quebec, which perhaps precluded obtaining big, prestigious commissions.

Despite these differences, there are several important factors shared by Canadian women architects across the country. Women architects from countries with established track records of women practitioners, especially in Eastern Europe, forced the doors of the associations open for Canadian-born women; many women architects from Quebec and the rest of Canada married architects (seven of eighteen in Quebec), and many of them established successful design partnerships with them. Finally, women architects from across Canada were clearly committed to practising and improving their chosen profession.

5

Unregistered Professionals: Women Redesign the Architectural Domain in Canada

Having argued in chapter 2 that women unregistered professionals have extended and elaborated upon the core areas of architectural practice, we turn, in this chapter, to a more detailed study of some of these women[1] and their careers. In particular, we are interested in influences that have propelled de-registered professionals towards non-masculinist careers, as well as in their reasons for reorienting their career trajectories. We profit from our data on men de-registered professionals in order to compare the experiences of Quebec women and men, and to underline the specificities of women's experiences as they extend the boundaries of the profession.

Before we turn to these questions, however, it is pertinent to outline the characteristics of the group of women de-registered professionals that we interviewed. As we mention in Appendix A, we constructed a stratified sample of respondents, drawn from the 1950s forward, to reflect all women de-registered professionals, over the research period, in terms both of their decade of entry and of the provincial associations with which they registered.[2] Some idea of the age range of our respondents can be derived from the fact that three obtained their first degrees in the 1940s, and eight in each of the 1950s/1960s, the 1970s, and the 1980s, thus reflecting architectural experience over the past fifty years.

We selected men de-registered professionals to match their Quebec women colleagues. Despite their being an even smaller sample, the Quebec men have experience of architecture over the 1970s, 1980s, and 1990s, which covers the experience of all but a couple of the Quebec women de-registered professionals. If we examine the year of first degree of the Quebec women and men only, we find (not surprisingly, given the later date of entry of Quebec women architects to the profession) that we have a younger group: four women (three men) have degrees from the 1950s/1960s, and fifteen women (seven men) from the

1970s/1980s. In brief, their experience is proportionally comparable. The interviews with both women and men took place over the period 1993–5.

With this brief introduction to our respondents, we turn to the questions raised at the beginning of this chapter: Why innovation? Why de-registration?

Why Innovation?

The first conclusion suggested by the data appears, at first glance, to be a firm one: The family background of de-registered women professionals provides minimal explanation for their innovative careers. If we think of mothers' occupations as an important influence on daughters' careers (e.g., Waite and Berryman 1985), more than half of our respondents' mothers worked solely as homemakers over most or all of their adult lives. Another third worked simultaneously in the so-called female occupations, while a small group of about half a dozen mothers undertook less traditional work. There appears to be little, at first glance, in the mothers' experience to explain their daughters' careers[3] – whether we are discussing the choice of architecture as a career or the decision to reject conformity to a strict professional mould.

If we look at fathers' occupations, on the other hand, frequently we find a professional background – over two-thirds of the fathers have a professional career as an engineer, a lawyer, a doctor, an accountant, or (in one case) an architect. Nearly two-fifths can be considered to have worked in the 'building trades' – as an engineer, builder,[4] or developer; in construction; or as an architect. Here, we detect some explanation of the choice of architecture as a profession, for a significant proportion of our respondents were brought up in a professional environment, and some of them, at least, were linked through their fathers to the building trades. In terms of socio-economic background, they were certainly influenced to pursue a university education and an appropriate profession – and architecture is not a surprising choice. But, once again, there is little explanation for innovation; on the contrary, their backgrounds suggest stable career orientations rather than change and innovation.

It is only when we examine the current family situation of respondents that some hints of a response to our question appear. Rather surprisingly, only one of our respondents has been single over her working career,[5] and four of her colleagues are no longer in a relationship (though a couple of them were in unions that lasted for as long as twenty-six years). Thus, a total of 19 per cent had no responsibilities, at the time of the interview, towards a spouse or partner. This pattern appears surprising in the context of professional women generally, and women architects in particular. Census data (table B.16 in Appendix B) show that a total of 37 per cent of female working architects were single, separated, divorced, or widowed as of 1991 – nearly double the proportion that we find among our respondents. Gwendolyn Wright (1977, 284) estimates that half the women architects of the 1970s were unmarried, and cites figures for 1920 which suggest that the proportion was nearer 75 per cent at that time. And, generally, the literature on professional women has acknowledged that one frequent method of 'coping' with the masculinist workplace has been to reduce domestic obligations – including to a partner.[6]

That our respondents are 'going against the grain' on this score is supported by data on children. Given their heavy responsibilities – to the workplace, to partners – it is surprising to find that a total of one-third of the respondents have three to five children, that is, notably more than is average for contemporary families.[7] Of all respondents, only four (or 15 per cent) have no children, but three of the four are graduates from the late 1980s who might yet decide to start families and, in fact, one of these respondents was pregnant at the time of the interview. Thus, it is not so much that the women have large families, but rather that they are not adopting the usual professional woman's approach of reducing family responsibilities, both to a spouse and to children.[8]

These quantitative data are rather surprising. Taken at face value, the propelling factor for innovation among these de-registered architects seems to be to find an alternative to the reduction of family responsibilities, that is, that domestic pressures have caused them, not to abandon the profession or to reduce domestic tasks, but to mould the profession around their private responsibilities. In effect, innovation as a strategy has replaced abdication and reduction. In contrast to one of our respondents in a previous research project who explained that she would not have children for she could only 'do two things well; have a good relationship with my husband and do very well in my career ...' (Tancred and Czarnocki 1993, 114), our de-registered architects have taken an alternative route. In effect, they have considered – and achieved – change in their workplace responsibilities, rather than radically reducing their private obligations.

In this context, the influence of the occupations of the mothers of respondents begins to take on a new importance. In keeping with the literature on this subject, mothers were possibly influential, for their homemaking careers appear to have had an impact on their daughters. In fact, the daughters may be continuing to observe the importance accorded by their mothers to domestic responsibilities – and this appears to have emerged in their choice of career trajectory, which is more of a fusion of the public/private domains than one might have anticipated.

Are there any further explanations for the nature of our respondents' careers in the background data? Once again, the data include elements that appear to go against the general tenor of the literature. For example, all our respondents have at least one university degree.[9] This proportion is, of course, higher than would be true of census data (table B.11) for, as of 1991, 82 per cent of women architects had a university degree. At the same time, this result is not surprising, as provincial associations have required a university degree for membership and our de-registered architects would have been obliged to comply.

What is perhaps surprising is that only four of our respondents (15 per cent) have a first degree in a field other than architecture,[10] yet Groat and Ahrentzen argue that nearly half (45 per cent) of their sample of faculty women in architecture received their first degrees in a discipline other than architecture (1997, 274). These authors argue that such a background predisposes faculty women to value a liberal education as a source of innovation and to 'make connections between architecture and many other disciplines' (p. 274). One might have hypothesized that a similar variety of educational backgrounds would be appropriate for the careers of our de-registered professionals as they branch out into new areas of endeavour – but this is not the case.[11] Thus, the nature of the first degree cannot be responsible for propelling our respondents towards an innovative career trajectory.

To complete the picture, however, it should be noted that about half our respondents have undertaken academic work outside architecture, often as a topic of a higher degree;[12] but these pursuits often occur just prior to the post-association career, and do not seem to be a reason for propelling the individual towards de-registered status, but rather a means of preparing them for such status. It should also be noted that three-quarters of Groat and Ahrentzen's sample, as compared with half of our sample, have at some time undertaken academic work in another field (1997, 275), thus maintaining the contrast in range of background disciplines between the two samples.

Thus, on the basis of a modest amount of quantitative data, it appears that our de-registered women are seeking out new career trajectories in order to combine fairly heavy domestic responsibilities with a continuing career.[13] Interestingly, they have chosen to modify workplace rather than personal responsibilities, thus contradicting most of the literature already cited on professional and managerial women. We sense some influence from rather traditional family origins – for these women from largely professional/homemaker families have oriented themselves towards a fusion of public and private careers and, in the process, have turned towards innovation.

Before we test these hypotheses against the interview data, let us turn briefly to material on Quebec women and men. Are there any contrasts between these two groups, and do these illuminate the tendencies outlined?

In brief, the Quebec women do not differ in terms of background from their colleagues across the country. They, also, are largely drawn from professional/ homemaker families, linked to a similar extent to the building trades. However, as we noted earlier, they are a younger group, and this factor is reflected in fewer family responsibilities; nearly 60 per cent have no children or only one child, but this makes little difference, as we shall see, to their reactions to the field of architecture. In terms of type and extent of qualifications, they reflect the general pattern outlined above – a first degree in architecture, from Quebec universities only, with a distinct propensity towards higher degrees, particularly for graduates from the 1960s and 1970s (78 per cent of them have higher degrees).

Fewer Quebec men, on the other hand, are drawn from professional (30 per cent)/homemaker (50 per cent) families; the fathers come from a wider range of occupations, including radar technician, railway worker, ranger, textiles salesperson, civil servant, publicist, mayor, and member of the provincial legislature. The link to the building trades is also less striking, and mothers' employment outside the home is limited to the 'female' occupations. The Quebec men are less qualified than their women colleagues; only 40 per cent have more than one degree, and only half of the graduates from the 1960s and 1970s have continued to higher studies. Compared with their women counterparts, a striking 40 per cent were educated outside Quebec, including Ontario; Chile; a combination of the former Soviet Union, Cambodia, and England; and Lebanon. All have first degrees in architecture.

It is difficult to characterize the careers of Quebec men and women; there are so many potential fields of employment that can be arranged in what appears to be an unending series of combinations. However, there are two ways in which the women and men differ significantly. First, the women experience a more tenuous attachment to the labour force, for they are much more likely to have worked part-time (37 per cent) than their male colleagues (10 per cent) at some period during their careers; the women are also more likely to have experienced periods of unemployment (30 per cent) than is true of their male colleagues (20 per cent).[14] There is little surprise in these results; census data (table B.12) have already informed us of the more tenuous nature of women's insertion into the labour force, and we know that part-time work is more characteristic of employed women than of men.[15] Given the mobile nature of these women's careers, however, one could argue that their insertion into the labour force is firmer than one might anticipate, for two-thirds of them have never experienced periods of unemployment.

The second difference between the genders is that the men have much more experience of self-employment (80 per cent) than do the women (5 per cent). Once again, this difference could have been anticipated on the basis of census data (table B.13), though the extent of the difference is rather astonishing. In fact, one suspects that self-employment replaces unemployment for the men,[16] that is, that they are able to set themselves up independently more easily than would be true of the women, who may not engender the trust from clients that independent status requires.

In brief, while the group of Quebec men is very limited in size, its members come from more varied ethnic and social backgrounds and possess fewer qualifications. For these reasons, they share a certain marginality with the women, though in their case, of course, such marginality is not based on gender. However, the Quebec men do not share certain career experiences of their women colleagues – in particular, they are less likely to work part-time. In addition, they are less likely to classify themselves as unemployed, and much more likely to claim the status of free-lancers or self-employed workers, though this is possibly a gendered difference in terminology, as suggested above.

The Innovation Process

Of course, the major question to be addressed concerning the innovation process is *why* the women (and men) respondents move from being registered to de-registered professionals. A preliminary comment is in order, and this concerns the significance of de-registration. All our respondents had, by definition, been members of provincial associations at some time during their career period. We, as researchers, however, were much more conscious of the exact dates of respondents' membership than they were – and could frequently remind them of these dates when memories faded![17] What became clear is that de-registration symbolized a certain stance vis-à-vis the profession, rather than a determination to move to a new career, and, in some instances, success in the relevant examination in order to become an association member was more important than registration.[18] In fact, the great majority of our respondents, as we shall report, did, indeed, move to a new career, but the timing did not necessarily coincide with de-registration. What is certain is that our respondents, by de-registering, effectively announced that they had no intention of moving steadily higher in the architectural firmament; instead, de-registration, for the great majority, presaged the type of innovation that we have been underlining throughout the presentation of our data.

The interview material is centred around the issue of *why* respondents chose to de-register and modify their career trajectories and, in fact, all of the questions asked during the interviews were directed, in one way or another, towards a more profound understanding of this process. Before entering into a discussion of the themes mentioned, it will be useful to specify that the overall

group of women and the subgroup of Quebec women do not differ significantly in the themes they raise (despite the age difference between the two
groups mentioned earlier). If anything, the Quebec women raise the same
themes even more strongly and more cohesively than do the national group,
and they add one minor theme that will be mentioned when we discuss differences between the Quebec women and men.

(a) 'Ce monde des affaires a la couleur des hommes qui n'est pas la nôtre'
    ('The business world has the colour of men which is not our own') (F:5)

The major theme raised by the women to account for their move to de-
registered status relates to the nature of the workplace and can be subsumed
under the eloquent formulation of one of our respondents: the workplace has
the 'colour' of men, to which women have no choice but to adapt. Under this
heading, our respondents discuss a wide range of topics. Among the most
important is the issue of schedules, for architectural work, as mentioned earlier, is characterized not only by long days and weekend work, but also by
haphazard schedules, accentuated by the increasing amount of 'contract' work
(F:8) that has characterized the profession in the recession phase. The repercussions on the personal lives of respondents are a constant theme. As one
respondent explains, child care on an irregular schedule is extremely difficult
to arrange and is enormously expensive: 'une gardienne qui est toujours dis-
ponible jusqu'à neuf heures puis quand ton patron a besoin de toi, se mon-
nayait assez cher quand même' ('a babysitter who is always available until
nine in the evening and when your boss needs you is fairly expensive') (F:10).
Another respondent talks of the concertina effect of available employment for,
'on travaille beaucoup, beaucoup pendant peu de semaines et après ça, on n'a
plus rien' ('you can work a lot, a lot over a few weeks, and after, there is nothing') (F:13); or as respondent F:2 phrases the point: 'I discovered that architecture work that you do on your own is sometimes very plentiful, and
sometimes doesn't exist.' An example of the ultimate in haphazard schedules
is provided by another respondent: 'mais ça m'est arrivé de me faire appeler le
lundi à 9h, je suis tout habillée, le manteau sur le dos: "Écoute, rentre pas,
c'est fini, on a plus besoin de toi."' ('On one occasion, they telephoned on
Monday at 9:00 A.M. I was all ready, with my coat on: "Look, don't come in;
the job is finished, we don't need you anymore"') (F:13).
    It is not merely a question of the extreme inconvenience of irregular sched-
ules for women who have simultaneous responsibilities within the home; the
women are by no means convinced that the schedules make sense. One
respondent comments on the cult of overtime that characterizes architectural

work: 'que les hommes ont cette mentalité de faire de "l'overtime," de "l'overtime," et de "l'overtime," alors que l'on sait très bien que dans n'importe quel milieu, et surtout en architecture, au bout de tant d'heures par semaine ou par jour, tu n'es plus rentable ... Pourquoi est-ce que les hommes persistent dans cette voie là?' ('men have this mental set of doing overtime, overtime, overtime, while it is well known in any setting, and particularly in architecture, that at the end of so many hours per week or per day, you are worthless ... Why do men persist in doing this?') (F:5). The brief answer of course, as Thomas points out in his study of corporate practices (cited in Ahrentzen and Groat 1992, 106), is that 'l'overtime' comes to have enormous symbolic value as managers substitute quantity for quality in their evaluation of work, and as time is used to signify dedication to work (Baker 1996, 14). The translation into the architectural domain, according to Cuff, is that the 'charette ethos' implies that good architecture requires work outside the official allotted time (1991, 70).

Some respondents are looking for more flexible schedules that facilitate the concentration of work in the evenings (F:13), or, more frequently, part-time work (F:5; F:22) and maternity leave (F:22), neither of which are readily available in this male-coloured architectural work world.

Running through the discussion of schedules is the theme of dependency. The women do not feel in control of their lives if they are to be buffeted by irregular schedules. But they also feel dependent in other ways. Respondent F:13 comments: 'Je suis toujours l'objet à la merci des gens ... On est comme des poupées où on se fait tout le temps manipuler par les gens ... Ça me tente pas d'être un pion qu'on manipule comme ça' ('I was always at the mercy of others ... We were like puppets that are constantly manipulated by others ... I don't want to be a pawn that is manipulated like that'). The causes of such dependency are, for example, that one is at the mercy of clients for 'the real world of clients intrudes on the freedom of designing' (F:14) or as another respondent, with her own firm, explains the relationship: 'Ils [les clients] peuvent te couper ... Tu leur as demandé $2,000 ... t'as beaucoup d'heures de travail ... ils veulent que tu le fasses pour $1,000; puis ils vont t'amener en cour' ('They [the clients] can cut you off ... You ask for $2,000 ... you have worked a great many hours ... they want you to do the job for $1,000; and they take you to court') (F:11). This relationship with clients does not only have financial consequences, but also influences one's freedom to design and to express one's ideas: 'ceux qui étaient les principaux ... ceux qui menaient l'affaire, c'était ceux qui avaient le cash ... et non pas ceux qui avaient les idées ... les designers sont vraiment pris pour des mouches ... T'arrives jamais à tes fins avec tes idées; elles sont toujours modifiées, tellement, que finalement il ne reste plus rien ('those who dominated ... those who led were those who had the money ... and not those who had the ideas. Designers are just seen as a lot of trouble ... You never manage to exploit your ideas fully; they are always modified, to such an extent that finally nothing is left') (F:18).

This leitmotif of the dominance of finances has a disillusioning impact on those trained to think of architecture as an artistic profession in which they would be able to express their creativity:

> Yea, I think there's disillusionment that comes to everybody because ... the whole thing is driven by money ... the client's money. A very experienced architect [who] was building models ... said to me: 'Well, sometimes on a project [if] you can get one handrail that you have designed that you are happy with, you've done really well, you know.' (F:19)

This disparity between expectations and what architects actually do has been documented in the literature on architects (Blau 1984, 54) and on the professions in general (Hughes, quoted in Cuff 1991, 45). This may not be a literature that is widely read by architectural students and practitioners; be that as it may, it is clear that the profession is much more successful at creating aesthetic expectations about architectural work than at conveying the nature of everyday practice to nascent architects (Baker 1996, 7).

The emphasis on financial exigencies manifests itself in extremely low remuneration, which is a central concern of many de-registered architects. Respondent F:4 termed her remuneration 'un salaire de crève faim' ('starvation wages'); another points out that it is possible to double one's remuneration in the public sector (F:10).[19] Many talk of feeling 'exploited' (F:9),[20] and they recognize that you reach a ceiling unless you establish your own firm (F:5).

Not surprisingly, respondents find that this context of 'just-in-time'[21] schedules and money-driven decisions does not encourage good working relations, and they often comment on the negative quality of interpersonal relations in the workplace. Respondent F:6 comments on stressful relations with 'le monde de la construction' ('the construction world') when doing on-site work, and the fact that she was never taken seriously if she was not accompanied by a man. Respondent F:18 talks about human relations in the workplace generally being very difficult: 'le respect des gens est très minime' ('respect for others is minimal'). Respondent F:11 states that she has found most architectural firms not to be very human working environments. Another respondent talks about being manipulated by her boss:

When he first introduced me to the developer ... he was quite supportive ... but probably he knew he could get his way with me ... He had a certain way of relating ... he would look at me in the eye ... a bit close ... not sort of sexual harassment close ... but more intimidation close ... he would ask me a question like, 'What's wrong?' or 'Why don't you want to work on this?' or 'What's the problem?' and then stare at me, intently, and not say a word ... I couldn't stand this tension ... Sometimes I felt that I was revealing too much of myself ... He was manipulating me. (F:9)

This respondent adds that, in general, firms were using women to 'glue' the office together or were just generally insensitive with respect to their employees.

Not surprisingly, this context of minimal respect for employees was translated into degrading task content for many of the women architects. They talk of the interesting aspects of design[22] being 'creamed off' by more senior members of the firm while they were relegated to routine work: 'I was tired of doing ... the working drawings ... it's awfully menial kind of work ... and the door schedule ... you have to make a list of every single door in the building and whether it's right-handed or left-handed' (F:9). Others talked about the fragmented nature of architectural work such that one never viewed the 'whole picture'; it was too much of a 'factory atmosphere' with 'a department for everything' (F:26). One respondent even talked of being relegated to the kind of work that no one else wanted to do: 'Je faisais les photocopies, je faisais les "blue prints"' ('I did the photocopies and the blue prints') (F:4). This is a far cry from our Quebec architects in chapter 4 who, in a context of opportunity, described very different architectural tasks and working environments.

This topic of the nature of architectural work and the working environment was the major focus when respondents discussed their move from registered to de-registered status; a total of 24 (or nearly 90 per cent) of the women respondents mentioned this topic from one perspective or another. In contrast to the frequent assumption that women's responsibilities in the private sphere propel them out of a male-dominated profession, this emphasis on the nature of the workplace is a far more frequent explanation in other studies as well, including the legal and academic professions, and management (Hagan and Kay 1995, 116; Tancred and Czarnocki 1998, 123; Rosin and Korabik 1991b, 327). In the current study, most of the comments were about working *conditions*[23] – haphazard schedules, dependent status, financially-motivated decisions, and minimal attention accorded work relations; however, these factors inevitably influenced the content of the work that the women architects were called upon to perform.

Overall, we get the impression of a group that is devalued by the architectural working environment. In being forced to fit into this male-coloured world, the respondents find that their need for a certain stability in order to take care of their responsibilities in the private sphere is given no consideration; as Kingsley and Glynn point out, 'the hesitancy to provide women with options such as flexible hours and day care ... is one of the most dangerous forms of discrimination against women' (1992, 17). In this sense, the architectural work context is totally discriminatory. In addition, the women's dignity as professionals is downplayed; the overt sexism that they describe relegates them to degrading and sometimes menial work. It is hardly surprising that one respondent reaches an extreme conclusion: '[L'expérience du travail] c'était pas du tout ... valorisant. Tu sais, les gens quand ils disaient: "Ah, tu es architecte, wow! Moi, je savais la réalité que je vivais ... Finalement, ce que je faisais, c'était rien' ('[The working experience] was not all ... positive. When people said: "Ah, you're an architect, wow!" I knew the kind of life I led ... Finally, what I did was nothing') (F:4).

(b) 'C'était un rythme assez essoufflant, très difficile' ('The pace was breathtaking, very difficult') (F:21)

As one explanation of the move from registered to de-registered status, we have separated out the issue of time demands on our respondents. In some ways, this could have been included as part of the previous theme and, in fact, the issue of overtime has already been raised. However, the topic includes not only the actual hours of architectural work, but also the whole constellation of time demands in the women's lives. For finally, the women delineate, perhaps better than feminist writings have been able to accomplish up to the present time, the ways that waged work, domestic work, and, possibly, some leisure time interpenetrate on a daily basis; they are constantly conscious of the articulation between their various uses of time, and the profound frustration that this causes in their private and public lives.

The second reason that this topic deserves separate treatment arises from a comparison between the women and the men. While this issue will be taken up in more detail in a later section, it is important to underline at this point that, whereas seventeen of the women (nearly two-thirds) mention this topic, *not one* of the men interviewed had any consciousness of conflicting, competing, and contradictory demands on his time. The reasons for this categorical contrast are fairly self-evident, though some subtleties require further discussion; but the contrast also legitimates the separate treatment of this topic.

As already suggested, the leitmotif running through the discussion of time demands is the articulation between or among competing demands. Respondent

F:10 talks, for example, of undertaking architectural work late into the evenings as well as on weekends – impossible hours when combined with child responsibilities. As respondent F:11 points out, evening and night work in architecture combined, with great difficulty, with renovations required for a new home she had purchased with her husband. Or as another respondent phrases it:

Quand on est architecte à la merci [du] patron ... quand il me dit de faire ça ... ça a des répercussions sur d'autres personnes après. Parce que Monsieur veut ceci, Monsieur veut ça ... je passe toute la fin de semaine au bureau pendant plusieurs semaines de temps; ... ils [la famille] vont dire: 'Qu'est-ce qui se passe? ... Maman, maman, je te vois jamais.' (F:13)

[When one is an architect at the mercy of the boss ... when he asks me to do something ... that has repercussions on other people. Because the Big Boss wants this or the Big Boss wants that ... I spend the whole weekend at the office over several weeks; [the family] then say: 'What's going on? Mummy, mummy, I never see you.']

Several of the respondents talk of the need for some space or free time in their schedules (e.g., F:2). Respondent F:21 talks about the difficulties in carrying out parallel work within and outside the home; she calls it a rhythm that left her 'breathless.' A graphic formulation is provided by respondent F:9: 'I felt constantly pressured by the time, time, time, time, time away from home, too much time on my studies, too much time at work ... I had no slack.' And the breathless aspect clearly permeates respondent F:5's description:

j'arrivais assez fatiguée et il y avait, bon ... faire à manger, faire le lavage, faire le ménage, s'occuper des devoirs, faire le bain ... Et les fins de semaine, le chalet. Les vendredis soir le lavage, l'épicerie, embarque dans l'auto, va au chalet, chauffe le chalet, couche le petit bébé. Le lendemain, le sport, le plein air, bon, ça arrête pas.

[I came home tired and I needed to ... make the supper, do the laundry, clean the house, supervise the homework, give [the baby] a bath ... And the weekends, the cottage. Friday evenings, the laundry, shopping, get into the car, go to the cottage, heat the cottage, put the baby to bed. The next day, sports, open-air activities; finally, there was no end to it.]

Clearly, respondents were propelled towards some sort of solution to these exhausting and contradictory demands. Respondent F:3 found a solution by 'just doing drawings for architects, which you could work part-time, still be within an office, still have some job satisfaction, but didn't have to be there day and night,' thus giving herself more flexibility. Those who turned to teaching often mention the 'fit' between their two schedules, of paid work and family work (e.g., F:22). Not the first woman to choose this solution, respondent F:19 talks about making a 'conscious decision ... [to] work with children in a school setting [teaching art], where I had more holidays and finished at 3:30 P.M. every day.' But the 'fit' is not merely with children's schedules; as respondent F:6 points out, teaching allowed her to arrange significant leave periods to travel with her husband, with the assurance that her job would await her on return. Family firms can also lessen the contradictory demands; as respondent F:1 indicates, when working for a family firm, she could 'call her own hours' such that she was home when her children returned from school.

This topic obviously reflects a continuing societal definition that women take the main responsibility for domestic work. Despite the fact that our respondents are, by definition, professional women, they do not question this domestic division of labour, nor do they make reference to the possible collaboration of their spouses or partners, partial though this might be. Given that our interviews were conducted in the 1990s in the context of extensive discussion of more egalitarian households, this is rather an astounding result. Admittedly, some of the women (though very few, as has been pointed out) were bringing up families on their own; but, for the great majority, the assistance of their male partners is noticeably absent when discussing demands on their time.

Hence, we see once again the influence of these women's families of origin, and particularly their mainly homemaker mothers, on the importance accorded to their family lives. Rather than requiring that their family obligations be changed, they are categorically oriented towards transformations in their workplace responsibilities. In some ways, the lack of change in the domestic sphere propels them towards much more radical demands in the public domain. It is, finally, a great irony, though completely logical, that the redesigning of the architectural workplace should be led by women whose private responsibilities appear to have responded little to the influences of social change within the home.

(c) 'Il fallait que je m'occupe de quelqu'un d'autre' ('I needed to look after someone else') (F:13)

The usual umbrella term 'family responsibilities' has little significance for our women respondents. When they talk about the domestic sphere, it is clear that they are talking about children. In addition, they sometimes make the distinction between one child and additional children as they think about the articulation between public and private work ('I quit definitely when I had the two children. I worked in between' [F:26]);[24] but spouses or partners are rarely mentioned, either as a resource, as indicated above, or as a responsibility within the private sphere.

What is the significance of children for our respondents? First and foremost, it is clear that they are seen as a responsibility in much the same way as professional responsibilities are defined: 'Tout d'un coup, je me rends compte que je n'avais pas seulement à m'occuper de moi, il fallait que je m'occupe de quelqu'un d'autre [le bébé] ...' ('Suddenly, I realized that I did not only need to look after myself. I also needed to look after someone else [the baby]') (F:13). This respondent clearly makes the distinction between a child-care responsibility and her obligations towards herself. Others verbalize this feeling in much the same way, either leaving out any mention of their partner, or making the distinction between the partner and their children. For example, respondent F:12 talks of the difficulty of combining motherhood with full-time work:

Q: This was a difficult combination, was it?
R: Yes ...
Q: Time?
R: Not so much time as guilt ... being a good mother.

Finally, she took four years to stay at home with her son. Her colleagues express similar thoughts: 'Je me sentais pas prête à me lancer pour devenir patron architecte avec un enfant' ('I didn't feel ready to aim for Principal status with a child') (F:10); 'J'avais deux enfants à ce moment-là ... je trouvais très difficile de faire, à la fois, tout le travail à la maison puis travailler en dehors' ('I had two children at that point ... I found it very difficult to do all the work within the home as well as work outside') (F:21).

There are also complexities related to child-care that are mentioned by respondents: 'Well, I figured we had just moved ... that was a big rupture for the kids and I needed to have more time with them' (F:24). Her colleague explains her withdrawal from her provincial association: 'My younger son is retarded; I was involved with [the] retarded association ... taking time to work with the association' (F:15). Another respondent voices similar preoccupations: 'Pour moi il y avait un souci épouvantable, c'étais que je voulais être aussi une bonne mère pour ma fille ... elle avait des problèmes à l'école ...

parce qu'elle vivait des traumatismes ... Elle est arrivée de la campagne à la ville avec sa mère seule alors qu'avant il y avait son père' ('For me, there was a major concern, which was that I also wanted to be a good mother to my daughter ... she had problems at school ... because she was going through some trauma ... She moved from the country to the city with her mother, whereas, formerly, there was also her father') (F:5).

Accompanying this image of devotion to motherhood is the joy and excitement of having children: 'Well, I'll tell you ... it was such an exciting thing to see a little human being develop that I didn't want to miss any of it' (F:26); and 'I could perfectly well have afforded a nanny when I first had them [the children], but I wouldn't have missed the experience of bringing them up for anything' (F:25).

Thus, in some ways, the nearly two-thirds (seventeen) of our women respondents who commented on their domestic responsibilities in some way *have* modified traditional responsibilities; they provide little evidence of responsibility *for* spouses or partners in the traditional sense of having to carry out any domestic work on their behalf.[25] On the other hand, they demonstrate a tremendous responsibility for, and enjoyment of, children.[26] This definition of the domestic sphere helps to explain their delineation of work in general; they clearly feel that their work within the home is equally, if not more important and responsible than their public-sector work. Both are clearly important components of their 'work.'

The fact that their spouses and partners come through the interviews as 'shadowy' figures is an interesting one;[27] they are in the background, though the vast majority of respondents are married or living with a partner. This result, at least in part, stems from the fact that the interviews focused on work, and we would certainly have gained a different image if we had centred our research on the family. But what the women are saying is that, as far as their working lives are concerned, their spouses and partners neither contribute to their responsibilities nor relieve them of significant responsibilities. These women are 'on their own' with respect to their work worlds.

(d) 'Mais qu'est-ce que j'ai foutu toutes ces années en architecture?' ('But what on earth was I doing in architecture for all those years?') (F:13)

Clearly, several of the women were attracted to new areas of architectural practice – and other endeavours – because of a certain interest inherent in the work. In some instances, these could be long-standing interests, dating back to university experiences, or more recent attractions growing out of their architectural experience. Just over half of the respondents (fifteen) explained their move to de-registered status by making reference to the attraction of new endeavours.

Respondent F:16 still remembers a critique of her work, done during her third year of architectural studies, which picked up on her interest in broader issues derived from her studies in art history. The invited critic told her: 'Tu ne seras jamais architecte; tu fais fausse route; ce qui t'intéresse, toi, c'est le design urbain' ('You'll never be an architect; you've got off on the wrong foot; it's urban design that you're interested in'). The respondent never forgot this advice, and went on to do a higher degree in urban planning and to work in this field. Another respondent talks of her early hesitations about architecture because of a strong interest in engineering; nevertheless, she completed the course and registered as an architect, only to return to her 'vieux rêve qui datait de plus de dix ans' ('long-standing dream over more than ten years') (F:21), undertaking both undergraduate and graduate studies in engineering.

But much more frequent than these early influences of alternative fields is the gradual realization on the part of many respondents that new avenues would be of greater interest for them. Thus, respondent F:13 talks of questioning her presence in architecture at one point and casually enrolling in art history courses. Eventually, she went on to complete a Master's degree in this field, saying to herself: 'Mais qu'est-ce que j'ai foutu toutes ces années en architecture? Là [en histoire de l'art], je me sens bien' ('But what on earth was I doing in architecture for all those years? In art history, I feel good'). Alternative trajectories took respondents from writing newspaper articles on architecture, on a part-time basis, to a career in architectural journalism (F:14); or accepting a job in planning, finding it interesting, and building a career in the area (F:2). Others, looking for ways to broaden their skills, either took an MBA and actively sought work in an exciting area of computer-aided design and data-base use, eventually leaving the field of architecture completely (F:12); or recognized that it was the 'structure and the technical side [of architecture] that I enjoyed more than the artistic side,' and thus, in this case, moving into three-dimensional work in sculpture, which turned out to be very satisfying (F:26). In brief, some dissatisfaction with the field of architecture was both illuminated and exacerbated by preliminary knowledge of alternative fields – and this led to major moves in career terms.

By definition, alternative avenues proved to be of greater interest than the traditionally defined domain of architecture for all our respondents. What is interesting in this set of data is that many were both pushed and pulled by the inherent aspects of both architecture and the preferred field; some recognized, or even unrecognized, discomfort with traditional architectural pursuits led to explorations and – in the main – innovative ways of employing architectural skills.

(e) 'Architects were driving taxis' (F:19)

Clearly, the personal experiences and preferences of the women interviewed were framed within the relevant economic conditions of their various career stages. While our respondents' experience covers approximately the last fifty years, all of them would have passed through recent recessionary phases and possibly other difficult periods in the post-war era. Many of them (thirteen, or nearly one-half) mention problems in obtaining employment in architecture. Respondent F:13, who had never planned to stop working when her children arrived, found that 'toutes les portes se ferment autour de moi' ('all the doors closed around me') when she tried to return after having her first child. Respondent F:14 found the situation for architectural practice to be 'dicey' and turned towards further studies; respondent F:2 found the market for architects to be more difficult than for planners – and directed her efforts in the latter direction. And throughout the interviews, we find comments that the situation was difficult in architecture because of the recession (F:4); that 'times are tough and you take what you can get' (F:7); 'the unemployment rate for architects ... was 50 per cent' (F:8); 'there is nothing being built' (F:1); 'there were no jobs for architects' (F:12); and 'the economy also took a downturn' (F:19).

Respondents were conscious that the social definition of architecture is that it is a 'luxury' rather than a necessity; Blau, for example, documents that only one-tenth of house construction at the period of her study in the United States involved an architect, as did only one-quarter of non-residential buildings (1984, 150, note 1). Kettle and Cohen, citing Canadian data from the mid-1950s, suggest that 55 per cent of housing was architect-designed at that time (or 'built from architects' plans,' as they carefully point out), 46 per cent of all single-family housing, 97 per cent of all apartment housing, and 100 per cent of all public housing (1958, 59). While the estimates are very difficult to make and Kettle and Cohen obviously find their data to be 'controversial,' what is clear is that professional architects have no legal or intrinsic monopoly over building design and, what is more, it is extremely easy to economize, in hard times, by using a builder's specifications/designs to avoid the architect's fee.

Despite the recognition of an unpropitious context for architectural employment at many points in the post-war period, the respondents also recognized that it was, indeed, possible to obtain architectural work and they had all, by definition, occupied such employment for varying career periods. Even in the hardest of times, they acknowledged a certain potential: 'J'en connais qui ont leur petit bureau privé, qui "tough," qui "tough," qui "tough," malgré le fait que les contrats ne rentrent pas facilement' ('I know some who have a small private office who "tough it out"; "tough it out" despite the fact that contracts are not easy to obtain') (F:16). Others express relief at the potential for stability in alternative employment, citing the guaranteed income that comes with a specialization in planning (F:2) or the advantages of the hospital sector, where there is always work (F:17). But the overwhelming relief on finding a 'real job' is palpable: 'I'm salaried and I've got a good income and I've got a company car and an expense account and ... it's a real job ... after five years, you have a pension plan, you know it's a real job. And this day and age, they're so hard to come by, and they're impossible to come by in architecture – and I mean impossible' (F:8).

Thus, we obtain an overall view of our respondents as struggling within a 'male-coloured' architectural work world, where they are largely devalued, accorded little dignity as professionals, and subjected to various forms of sexism. As their responsibilities in the private and public spheres accumulate, the women provide evidence of 'breathless' schedules and of little assistance from partners or spouses. The economic context is not propitious for employment in the architectural field, and they are frequently attracted by new fields because of long-standing or recent interests. This combination of factors has, by definition, propelled them into 'alternative employment,' following de-registration from their provincial associations, though, as we have already seen, the vast majority of such employment has strong links with architecture.

With this image of our women de-registered professionals, we turn briefly to a comparison between the women and men interviewed. It should be remembered that the Quebec women do not differ profoundly from their national colleagues in their interview responses though they are younger; thus the following section contrasts the Quebec men's experience with the general image of the women delineated above.

Gender Differences: Innovation and De-registration

A comparison between the Quebec women and men leads to strong statements about the ways in which they are *dissimilar*. As mentioned earlier, not one of the men made any mention of the time taken up by architectural employment; there are no accounts of impossible schedules, and no concerns about how to fit together their public and private responsibilities. In fact, if the spouses/partners of our women respondents are in the shadows, the spouses/partners of our men respondents are non-existent, as the men talk about their public-only work responsibilities. Quite logically, then, not one of the men talked about being attracted by better schedules in his new employment, and no one mentioned wanting to spend more time with his family. Time is just not a factor for these male de-registered architects.

Working conditions generally play a lesser role in the consciousness of our male respondents. Not only is there no mention of gender discrimination, but not one of the men cites the health consequences of his working schedules. This issue is, admittedly, raised by a small minority of the Quebec women, but is still present – stress and burnout, crippling arthritis, back problems, and difficulties with vision being cited by the few women who mention this topic. Clearly this is not part of the male experience.[28]

Thus, if dual responsibilities to the private and public spheres and the resulting time pressure affect none of the men, how do they explain their reasons for de-registering from the architectural profession? Their main reason parallels that of the women, but is interpreted in a particular fashion. Basically, the men indicate a distancing and an alienation from the domain of architecture which takes them into alternative work. Respondent M:1 talks about the profession not being 'present' in his life: 'Même à l'école, je sentais que c'était pas très présent, parce que j'étais toujours spatial ... ça ne 'clique' pas' ('Even at school, I felt that it wasn't too present because I was always spatially inclined ... it doesn't "click"'). His colleague talks about being 'disillusioned,' saying 'I lost interest at that point' (M:2). Respondent M:3 claims that the interior architecture of Quebec is much richer than the exterior, because of the extreme cold: 'Moi, je suis urbaniste ... j'ai un petit peu des contraintes ... mentales pour travailler en architecture' ('I am an urbanist ... I have sort of mental limits about working in architecture'). Respondent M:4 indicates that he does not find architecture sufficiently challenging, and a colleague argues that aesthetics are irrelevant in architecture and that he needs to be creative (M:6).

The final respondents do mention client control – a theme mentioned by the women earlier – and the consequences for their lack of 'integrity' (M:7), jobs rather than a career (M:8), and projects stripped of any interest by client pressures (M:9). But they are very specific about *how* they want to work, while simultaneously joining the women in recognizing the source of the constraints.

This very specific definition of their interests and strengths carries through into their discussion of what attracts them to alternative employment. Respondent M:4 talks about 'la piqûre de la construction' ('the call of construction'), of how much more exciting it was, noting that it offered a much better future. Another respondent recounts how his experience of project management gave him an interest in the nature of organizations and how they work – and this took him into work in management (M:6). For a couple of respondents (M:3; M:7), urbanism became an attraction, with its territorial dimensions, emphasis on neighbourhoods, and 'Garden Cities.' Another respondent 'fell in love with the computer business' and, on being complimented on his way of explaining relevant computer material to his technician, gradually moved into teaching in the community-college sector (M:9). Perhaps the best account comes from one de-registered architect who decided to do graduate work in mathematics, and thus to leave architecture altogether; he describes in great detail how an interest in geometry led him into architecture – and how he built a model of a shape 'that to me has so much potential that it was like an obsession ... when I got to a certain point, I just couldn't go any further with it ... I decided that I wanted to learn general mathematics ... to be able to decide how to explore this thing further' (M:2).

In all these cases, the respondents were able to articulate their personal 'love affair' or 'obsession' or 'piqûre' with a particular approach to work[29] that could not be satisfied within traditional architectural practice, and that led them to new avenues of study and employment. In addition, some of them talk about the chance to improve their skills, which is coherent with this interest in differing approaches to work. In brief, their critique is much more an expression of how *they* think architecture should be practised; they are the mavericks and the rebels of architecture (M:2), in the sense of disagreeing profoundly with the approach inherent in the practice of architecture. As square pegs in round architectural holes, they eventually work their way out into more satisfactory working contexts. But they are not particularly innovative in the use of their skills; rather, they seek a context (construction, more flexible architectural employment) where *their* definition of architecture can find expression.

Obviously, the approach inherent in architectural work was not the only reason for changing the type of employment; the men also make reference to economic downturns, and they accord more importance than the women to very low salaries and the financial advantages of alternative employment.[30] But none of these accounts has the same passion, the same propelling force, as their discussion of new approaches to work; the men are clearly driven by their rebellious definition of what excites or interests them in work, and this led to alternative avenues of employment.

Reinterpreting the 'Mommy Track'?

We end with this contrasting image of women and men de-registered architects. The women are propelled by an overwhelming working context to experiment with the use of their architectural skills in alternative domains; the men express their maverick definition of the field by moving to connected work contexts where they have greater freedom to express their personal viewpoints on architectural or alternative practice. For women, as suggested by census data (tables 2.3A and 2.3B), de-registration leads towards extending the frontiers of the architectural profession, for the most part; for men, de-registration is linked to their personal redefinition of ways of working within or outside architectural practice.

The question that remains concerns the women. If we are arguing that de-registered women have explored alternative forms of employment, where the great majority can still utilize their architectural skills while simultaneously taking care of extensive domestic responsibilities, are we not merely categorizing those who follow the so-called mommy track[31] under a different heading? Are our women not just in the process of translating the 'mommy track' within a professional context, where career trajectories are more varied and less organizationally constrained?

In some ways, the answer must be positive. Our women respondents, as has been discussed, are propelled by a fusion of public/private responsibilities to mould the former around the latter. They are demanding that this fusion of public and private workplaces be coherent, tolerable, and humane. While remaining within the contours of architectural work, they have carved out innovative public responsibilities that utilize their architectural skills, while still leaving space for private responsibilities.

This said, it should be recognized that expressions such as the 'mommy track' and variants have been created by men in the public workplace. Because male occupants of professional positions have not needed to knit together a range of work responsibilities, the focus on their public responsibilities has dominated the male-coloured work world. From women's perspective, the so-called normal track is totally abnormal; it makes demands of the professional worker that can be fulfilled only if domestic responsibilities are limited by childlessness, or if the major part of domestic responsibilities is hived off from public ones and undertaken by a separate worker. Yet, our women respondents are arguing that this is not the way they wish to live their domestic experience; they aim for a humane combination of work responsibilities that would give them an acceptable schedule, with time included for leisure activities.

From women's perspective, the 'normal track' has little to recommend it, as it centres on heavy workplace responsibilities, divided from domestic relations and work. It is the track of insanity rather than normality, as professionals scramble to pack an impossible series of tasks into normal working hours – taking refuge in 'l'overtime' on an unending basis in order to accomplish the impossible. In this context, the 'mommy track' becomes the 'fusion track,' where some balance can be maintained between public and private responsibilities. The women have worked very hard to create such a track and their innovative practices result from this concern for balance.

For the women still consider themselves to be architects – that is clear. As respondents express it: 'I'll always be an architect ... [I] don't have to practise' (F:14); 'Je suis de coeur ... avec les architectes' ('My heart is ... with the architects') (F:16); 'I'm speaking as an architect' (F:3); 'I don't need their [the association's] recognition to feel like I'm a "capable architect"' (F:20); 'Yes, I do [consider myself to be an architect] because ... I have an appreciation of things because of my training and ... experience and, yes I do very much' (F:28); and 'Moi, je me sens architecte à la base' ('I am fundamentally an architect') (F:18).[32]

There are naturally some regrets that architectural practice could not accommodate their fused responsibilities. Many would like to be in architectural practice if their domestic responsibilities could be accommodated. Others express a continuing interest in and commitment towards specific aspects of architecture as a field – design, 'the aesthetic part,' 'une interdisciplinarité' ('a certain interdisciplinarity'). It is rare for respondents to express negative reactions towards architecture.[33] At the same time, the current form of architectural practice is another matter, as the analysis has indicated.

Very few respondents criticized their current employment; these career paths have been chosen and actively pursued. This employment is not male-defined architectural practice, but it enables them to deal with their varying responsibilities and, for the vast majority, to simultaneously work with their architectural skills. The 'fusion track' is both satisfying and creative – in the sense of architectural skills and with respect to the profession in general.

6

The Quebec Question: Designing a Distinct Experience

Throughout our study of Canadian women architects, we have been intrigued by differences between Quebec women architects and those in the rest of Canada. Together with our colleagues from various disciplines who are interested in the specificity of this mainly francophone province, our initial reaction was to pose this question: What explanation can we offer for differences between the Quebec women architects and their women colleagues in the rest of Canada? However, on further reflection, we conclude that such a question is framed, rather ironically, within an implicit discourse of similarity rather than difference. It implies that Quebec women ought to have achieved the same stages at similar moments as their counterparts in the other provinces. As we argue later in this chapter, such a discourse is inappropriate. Instead, we look, in this discussion, for explanations of the specific pattern of experience that characterizes our Quebec women architects. As will become clear as the chapter progresses, we hypothesize, first, that Quebec women architects have come to the fore in a context of tremendous social upheaval. This hypothesis does not deny a period of major social change in the other Canadian provinces (see, for example Parr 1995, 3ff., on Ontario). However, as will become evident in the succeeding sections, we are arguing that Quebec's experience differed in *degree,* that is, that social changes which took much longer in the other provinces were accelerated into a relatively brief period in the Quebec case. Obviously, our hypothesis could be applied to the experience of women architects in the rest of Canada, for there is no doubt that they entered the profession during a period of social change; but Quebec becomes an 'extreme case' scenario where changes took place at an overwhelming pace. The so-called Quiet Revolution[1] was indeed just that – a plethora of concurrent social transformations rarely experienced in a peacetime context.

Our second hypothesis raises the possibility that the so-called Continental model has influenced Quebec women architects to take the lead in developing a parallel practice to the official profession of architecture. As we will explain later in the chapter, we hypothesize that the cultural contacts with continental Europe, which are more frequent for francophones who dominate Quebec than for anglophones who dominate the other provinces, have encouraged both a different manner of obtaining access to architectural practice and a new way of practising the profession in general.

The Quebec Experience

Let us briefly outline the specific pattern demonstrated by our Quebec women architects. As the material in previous chapters indicates, Quebec women were later (1942) entrants to their professional association than their colleagues in the rest of Canada (1925). However, as of the 1970s, all subsequent developments took place at a breakneck pace. If we look at women registrants over the research period (1920–92), 53 per cent of all Canadian women registrants were drawn from Quebec (table B.7). Not surprisingly, the results of this massive influx of Quebec women are reflected in Quebec women's current presence within the profession; as of 1992, 55 per cent of all Canadian women registered architects were members of the Quebec association (table B.8). In brief, over the short decade and a half from 1971 to 1986, Quebec women registered architects not only caught up with their Canadian colleagues, but overtook them – significantly – in terms of their presence within the profession.

Census data, covering all architects, demonstrate less dramatic rates of growth in the inclusion of Quebec women; as of 1991, 34 per cent of all women architects are drawn from Quebec, while 36 per cent are drawn from Ontario (table B.9). What is clear from the comparison of association and census data, and as we know from our own material, Quebec women have been registering in greater numbers than their colleagues elsewhere in Canada; they easily dominate the category of registered women architects while 'more than taking their place,'[2] at approximately one-third of women architects, when both registered and unregistered architects are included.

While Quebec women architects may have registered in greater numbers, they have also exited their association more rapidly than their colleagues elsewhere in Canada. Over the total research period, their rate of exit is one and a half times that of their Ontario colleagues (table 2.4).[3] Not surprisingly on the basis of this figure, Quebec women constitute a clear majority (54 per cent) of all women exiting from provincial architectural associations. However, as we have noted, despite this high rate of exit, Quebec women still dominate registered female architectural practice in Canada as of 1992.[4]

This overall sketch indicates a great deal of movement on the part of Quebec women architects. Over a period of five decades (1942–92), they have come to parallel their Canadian colleagues in terms of the number who self-identify as architects, presumably on the basis of relevant qualifications. Over an even shorter period (1942–86), they have literally taken over female registered architectural practice in Canada; in effect, they have invaded their professional association to such an extent that, despite a high rate of de-registration, as of the 1990s they still maintain their numerical dominance over the some 850 women within the profession in Canada. In effect, in terms of presence within the profession, they have concentrated into the post-war period what Canadian women architects in the other provinces have yet to accomplish, despite their earlier starting date.

But as we indicated in chapter 4, their contributions to the profession have not only stemmed from their numerical presence. Quebec women architects, or those who started out in Quebec, are notable for their work on high-profile, non-residential projects, thus negating the general image of housing, interiors, and historical preservation as the appropriate domains for women. Indeed, Quebec women have worked on multi-use blocks, banks, major expositions, and even whole sections of cities. They became noted specialists of hospitals and school designs. As pointed out earlier, they have built 'megacareers' on the foundation of 'megastructures.' Thus, not only is the Quebec woman architect a 'woman in a hurry,' she has also more than made her contribution to important fields and approaches to architecture.

In keeping with the approach outlined at the beginning of this chapter, we submit that it would have been surprising if Quebec women architects and their Canadian colleagues had followed a similar pattern. In particular, we hypothesize (along with Rossiter 1978, Mitchell 1986, Collin 1992, and others),[5] that women in general come to the fore in times of turbulence and major social upheaval; that they are encouraged to experiment in contexts of transformation; and that they take the risks inherent in new social conjunctures. Catherine Chard Wisnicki, McGill's first woman graduate in architecture, expresses a similar theme: 'I anticipate a great future for women in architecture, particularly in view of all the current upheavals in society. It is my contention that women are awfully good at dealing with upheavals.'[6]

We acknowledge that the exact formulation of our first hypothesis for the explanation of the Quebec 'experience' differs slightly from that of previous authors. For example, Mitchell phrases her hypothesis as follows: 'My tentative hypothesis is that women are used within the economy as a temporary advance guard or, perhaps, as a toe in the water of an unknown sea' (1986, 36). Rossiter, concerned with the entry of women to the scientific fields, underlines a pragmatic aspect: 'in a rapidly growing field, with a shortage of highly qualified people, women would be tolerated, and even sought out ... since they would typically be paid lower salaries than men' (1978, 147). And, finally, Collin, in her study of Quebec pharmacists, insists: 'La féminisation interviendrait donc à des moment clés de changements dans l'organisation du travail' ('Thus, feminization occurs at key moments in the changing organization of work') (1992, 36) and that women occupy 'de nouveaux postes créés dans la foulée des transformations qui se produisent' ('new positions created within the context of multiple changes') (p. 50). However, running through these formulations can be noted the emphasis on social change and transformation, and the innovative experience of women within such a context;[7] our hypothesis becomes a generalization of these various formulations.

If our hypothesis is, indeed, correct, how could our Quebec women architects have been excluded from the transformatory experiences characterizing Quebec in the post-1940 and particularly the post-1960 period? Why should they be more similar to their architectural colleagues elsewhere in Canada than to the women of Quebec with whom they shared this period of massive social upheaval? It is to a discussion of their women colleagues and of the context of social change within Quebec that we now turn.

Quebec Women at the Frontiers

To put our women architects in context, let us underline that they were by no means alone in the type of pattern we have delineated above. In effect, this pattern of a late start followed by take-off,[8] which overtakes the achievements of their colleagues from anglophone provinces, characterizes Quebec women in several domains. On the subject of a late start, Marianne Ainley contrasts the experience of anglophone women who obtained higher degrees in the sciences in most Canadian universities after the First World War, with that of francophone women who did not carry out parallel work until the 1950s (1996, 5). Micheline Dumont (1992, 77) has several examples: that English-Canadian women gained access to universities 'shortly after 1850,' Quebec women in 1907;[9] that the right to own property was accorded to married women in 1872 in English Canada and, following several amendments to the Civil Code, in 1964 in Quebec; that the first feminist movements were organized in Canada around 1880 and in Quebec in 1907; and, finally – how could one forget? – that Canadian women gained the right to vote federally in 1918, whereas Quebec women had to wait for 1940 to vote at the provincial level.

As suggested earlier, this issue of Quebec 'lateness'[10] is usually approached

as if other provinces provide a desirable standard for various 'achievements.'
For example, Dumont indicates that Quebec's 'lateness seems all too evident'
(1992), without raising the issue as to whether the significance of such rights
and stages was the same for Quebec women as for those in the rest of Canada.
However, this issue is raised with respect to the provincial vote for Quebec
women by various scholars. As the Collectif Clio points out, the vote for
women at the provincial level was obtained during the Second World War and,
while it might have been expected to symbolize 'leur entrée définitive dans la
vie publique ...' ('their definitive entry into public life'), Quebec women were
too caught up with the effects of the war to pay much attention to this change
in their status (1992, 373). In contrast to the strong suffragist movement that
surrounded the struggle for the vote in the rest of Canada, this rather casual
stance with respect to the vote on the part of a large number of women in Quebec is striking.[11] Given the local circumstances, why should they have
obtained the provincial vote at the same time as in the anglophone provinces?
In its 'lateness,' Quebec was more in line with other Civil Code jurisdictions,
such as France and Switzerland, than with Anglo-Celtic countries. In a similar
vein, why should the experiences of Quebec women in general occur at the
same time as those of their counterparts in the rest of Canada?

As to the 'take-off' that succeeded the vote, this comes through very clearly
in the political presence of Quebec women in the post-1960 period. Once
again, the initial date is 'late' in comparison with the anglophone provinces,
but, in 1961, Claire Kirkland-Casgrain became the first woman member of the
Quebec provincial legislature (Collectif Clio 1992, 441). The sequel comes
rapidly; by 1984, half of the female members of the Canadian House of Com-
mons came from Quebec, which includes about one-quarter of the Canadian
population (though this representation was reduced to 33 per cent in 1988)
and, by 1989, Quebec had more women members in the provincial legislature
than any other province (Dumont 1992, 78). It is interesting to note that, also
by the mid-1980s, Quebec women architects had overtaken their colleagues
elsewhere in Canada and had come to dominate female practice within Canadian architecture.

A similar 'take-off' pattern is apparent in what might be considered the professions that are 'parallel' to architecture (cf. chapter 1). As far as dentists,
engineers, lawyers, and physicians are concerned, as of 1961 Quebec women
manifested a lower-than-average or merely average presence within the profession of their province; by 1986, they had attained a percentage that was
well beyond the average for the profession in Canada (tables B.1–B.4).[12] If we
limit comparisons to the two largest provinces (Ontario and Quebec), where
absolute numbers are more than sufficient for viable comparisons, the pattern

is clear. As of 1961, the proportion of Quebec women in all of the above professions was equal to (engineers) or well below (the other professions) the
proportion of Ontario women whereas by 1986, the Québécoises had out-
stripped their Ontario colleagues significantly and *always* manifested a higher
proportion of women than in the neighbouring province.[13] The statistical
'turning points' vary from the early 1970s (law and engineering) to the mid-
1970s (dentistry and architecture) to the early 1980s (medicine), reflecting, of
course, the social changes that had taken place a few years earlier. Thus,
within a maximum of twenty years, these women professionals in Quebec
overtook their sisters from Ontario in terms of their representation within each
of these professions.

Thus, we argue that Quebec women architects resemble their women colleagues within the province rather than their female architectural colleagues in
the rest of Canada in terms of the pattern of their participation in the profession. However, such a statement begs the question: Why were Quebec women,
in general, at the frontiers at this particular time? As suggested above, we are
delineating a context of social turbulence, particularly from the 1960s forward, which channelled the talents of Quebec women towards new positions
within their changing society. As to major social change, there is ample evidence for this; as the Collectif Clio points out, the death of Premier Maurice
Duplessis in 1959, and the defeat of his ultra-conservative Union Nationale
party in the ensuing elections in 1960, mark the start of the so-called Quiet
Revolution in Quebec (1992, 441). Over the next decade and a half, the
province passed from a right-wing conservative government to a nationalist/
separatist government, the Parti Québécois, which first came to power in
1976. This political upheaval reflected major social and economic changes,
not least of which was the massive decrease in the farming population, which
dropped by more than 50 per cent over the period from 1961 to 1976 (Linteau
et al. 1991, 359).

The influence of the Catholic Church waned considerably over the 1960s:
'The changes that took place in a span of ten years were fundamental: the
Catholic hierarchy lost its decision-making power in education; priests and
religious [personnel] dwindled in numbers and gradually disappeared from
Quebec's schools, colleges and hospitals ...' (Linteau et al. 1991, 476). Attendance at mass dropped dramatically over the 1960s. In Montreal alone, the
decade 1961–71 marked a decrease of attendance from 61 per cent to 30 per
cent in the Montreal diocese; by the end of the 1970s, attendance varied
between 37 and 45 per cent for Quebec Catholics as a whole (McRoberts
1988, 139). Coherent with these changes was the dramatic decline in the birth
rate; from 1959 to 1969, the birth rate decreased by 50 per cent, 'a change that

in the rest of the country took place over the span of a century. By 1970 Quebec had the lowest birth rate of any of the provinces (15 per 1000)' (Prentice et al. 1988, 321–2).

As far as the educational system was concerned, the provincial Ministry of Education slogan 'Qui s'instruit s'enrichit' ('Education brings wealth') accompanied a whole succession of reforms: 'While in 1971 only 57.7% of the population fifteen and over had completed grade nine, in 1981 the figure was 73.6 percent' (Linteau et al. 1991, 493). University access mushroomed; over the five-year period from 1966 to 1970, 'there were more university graduates than in the ten preceding years ...' (p. 488).

The economic structure was simultaneously transformed. Over the period of the Quiet Revolution, Quebec saw the rising dominance of the public sector and of small and medium-sized firms, such that economic power within the province passed from anglophones to francophones. Over the 1960s, the provincial and municipal governments invested massively in the construction of government buildings, schools, and road systems, to say nothing of massive public projects such as the Montreal metro, which opened in 1966; the world fair, Expo 67; and the Manicouagan 5 dam, which opened in 1968 (p. 309).

These are merely a few examples of the extent of the concentrated changes over the 1960s and 1970s in Quebec.[14] While commentators recognize that many of these changes had their roots in the post-war period, the rapidity of change that was encapsulated within the period of the 'Quiet Revolution' cannot be denied. Comments on this topic are all too clear: as Dickinson and Young point out, the demographic evolution in Quebec included 'phenomena [which] are common to the western world, [but] the shifts in Quebec have been more dramatic' (1993, 294); McRoberts refers to the 1960s as a period when the beliefs and assumptions of over a century were abandoned (1988, 128); Prentice et al. note that, into the 1960s, 'French-Canadian women were experiencing demographic and economic transformations even more dramatic than those affecting other Canadian women' (1988, 328). It was not so much that the province was experiencing a different kind of social transformation; rather, changes that had taken place elsewhere at an earlier period were concentrated, at a remarkable pace, into this period of about two decades, which has, justifiably, come to be viewed as a period of revolution.

However, with our Quebec women architects, we are witnessing women not only entering a profession at breakneck pace, but also practising the profession in an innovative fashion; and this in at least two ways. First, as amply illustrated in chapter 4, Quebec women registered architects have taken the lead in a wide variety of architectural arenas, contributing not only to major projects within the province (and elsewhere), but also to the very parameters of architectural practice by taking a lead role in the development of Modernism in Canadian architecture. Second, as has been mentioned, Quebec women not only dominate, both numerically and in terms of their type of approach, registered female architectural practice in Canada, but also de-registered female architectural practice. As we have argued throughout this volume, it appears that the vast majority of de-registered architects are using their architectural qualifications in an innovative fashion – and we have described the wide range of subsequent employment among our sample of de-registered architects, which supports this argument.

How can we explain Quebec women's innovations within architectural practice? To some extent, the Rossiter hypothesis, cited above, explains the inclusion of Quebec women architects within the profession in the post-1960 period, for the province was making demands of its provincial architects to participate in major self-affirmatory projects such as Expo 67; the megastructured Place Bonaventure, also completed in 1967; the mixed-use urban development of La Cité, which opened for the 1976 Olympics; not to mention a general participation in major urban-planning projects. The need for architectural expertise was evident – going well beyond any general requirements of post-war expansion. As we have pointed out (chapter 4), the projects required the skills of risk-takers – La Cité, for example, was a 'hot potato' that had already been refused by male architects; Place Bonaventure experimented with a much more interactive design process; the scale of Expo 67, by definition a once-only project, was undoubtedly a life-changing experience. Mitchell's hypothesis about women acting as a 'temporary advance guard' clearly fits this type of practice among Quebec women architects of the 1960s and early 1970s.

But our hypothesis of women's role within a transformatory social context is not as helpful, at first glance, for de-registered architectural practice. For one thing, de-registration among Quebec women architects is a later phenomenon, of the late 1970s and 1980s, rather than of the preceding fifteen-year period.[15] Was this a period of disillusionment for practising women architects? Our interviews with de-registered Quebec women architects provide no image of women who left burgeoning careers in order to construct alternative employment. There were certainly some women who had worked on interesting projects for short time periods, but the lack of seniority of most of the women interviewed – under eight years for most of them (see table 2.5B)[16] – would have prevented their taking responsibility for megaprojects comparable to those of their colleagues of the 1960s.

And, in fact, this issue of expanding the arena of practice is a major clue for our de-registered architects. In brief, architectural practice over the post-1975 period was no longer located within a time of massive social opportunity. The 1973 oil crisis had its repercussions on the Quebec economy and, with the election of the Parti Québécois in 1976, the attention of the province turned increasingly to projects oriented towards independence. The recession of the early 1980s marked a period of restricted opportunity in all domains, including new construction projects. The period of revolution, affirmation, and innovation had passed.

But Quebec women continued to enter the architectural profession in massive numbers; a total of 83 per cent of all Quebec registered women entered their provincial association between 1980 and 1992, that is, during the final thirteen-year period of our research (table B.7). But as we have already outlined, they also de-registered in significant proportions, not sufficient to lose their status as the dominating provincial group of women architects within Canada, but sufficient to dominate all women de-registering from provincial associations. What has been going on over this recent period, from about the early 1980s forward?

Returning to our argument throughout this volume, we must respond that the Quebec women architects uncovered a new means of participation. In a significant proportion of cases, as discussed in chapter 5, they acquired their qualifications, passed the professional examination in order to become registered architects, and took a considered look at contemporary architectural practice; they then severed their ties with official practice. As we know, the great majority of women branched out into 'unofficial' architectural practice; teaching; and the arts; as well as a wide range of idiosyncratic employment linked to architecture (chapter 2). Their innovation, we have argued, is that they uncovered a greater variety of ways to use their architectural qualifications. In so doing, we recognize that they are demonstrating a form of practice that is familiar in European contexts (see the discussion of the 'Continental' model in the next section). However, the point is that they are underlining a form of practice that is innovative for Canada, thus creating what we have termed 'fused' careers, bringing together both their public and their private work.

The major contrast between the Quiet Revolution and subsequent decades is that, in the initial period, women were needed and welcomed into the profession, where they occupied frontier positions *within* the profession; in the later period, women have created their own positions at the frontiers of the whole profession of architecture. In both instances, we submit that, in contrast to arguments about their marginality to the profession, they have carved out new arenas of practice, at the frontiers of both the 'official' and 'unofficial' architectural domains.

Quebec Women Architects and Professional Women

Our understanding of Quebec women architects is located within the provincial context. We have argued that their experience is very similar to that of their colleagues in other domains within the province; that it can be comprehended on the basis of the various waves of social change that swept over their province during the Quiet Revolution; that Quebec women architects more than 'took their place' at the frontiers of the profession at a period of provincial self-affirmation and opportunity; and that, since the 1980s in particular, they have also taken their place at the frontiers of 'unofficial' architectural practice.

It is with respect to unofficial practice that we would like to make some final comments. First, it is clear (cf. chapter 2, note 37) that the whole notion of unofficial practice rests on a commonality of qualifications. By definition, all our de-registered architects have completed both tertiary-level and professional qualifications in order to become registered architects, and these qualifications accompanied them into unofficial practice. Savage has argued that women are much more likely to pursue occupational rather than organizational careers (1992, 131); we would modify this statement to say that women often establish wide-ranging careers on the basis of educational qualifications rather than organizational experience. In effect, our de-registered women are firmly rooted in their architectural qualifications, which they then employ in a wide range of alternative capacities.

This statement is consistent with an observation by Burrage, Jarausch, and Siegrist in their comprehensive work *Professions in Theory and History*, where they state: 'it would appear that professions where entry is practitioner-controlled are least accessible to women, and correspondingly those where entry is controlled by universities or by the state are more open to them' (1990, 223).[17] These authors are, of course, making reference in the first instance to the so-called Anglo-American and, in the second, to the Continental model of the professions (cf. also Buchner-Jeziorska and Evetts 1997, 63ff.), where the first refers to the professions (as in Canada) that are controlled by their professional associations, which set down entry regulations and specify the required educational background, exams, and apprenticeship period, as appropriate. The profession is thereby under the jurisdiction of those who have already gained access, and who inevitably seek to ensure as much similarity of background as possible among new recruits.[18]

The second, 'Continental,' model refers to European practice, where the state and/or tertiary-level institutions, by admitting candidates to an educational institution, in effect provide access to the relevant profession (Holmwood and Siltanen 1994/5, 47ff.). The classic example of the latter is, of course, French practice where admission to the prestigious 'Grandes Écoles,' controlled by the state, in the fields of engineering, management, public administration, and so forth, thereby provides access to the pertinent professions. Since educational institutions, whether state-controlled or not, have been more 'open' to women than professional associations, it has been easier, as Burrage et al. point out, for women to enter a profession by the former rather than the latter portal. Such commentators are generally concerned with the greater ease of *access* for women, but the 'Continental' model can also imply different modalities of *practice*, as we know from the many European architects who branch out into a variety of fields.[19]

What do these comments have to do with the 'unofficial practice' of our women architects? We come to our second hypothesis: that one can envisage these careers as an attempt to delineate a 'Continental' model of the profession in parallel to the existing 'Anglo-American' one. Since these women are using their education as the basis of their subsequent careers, they are following a model in which educational qualifications are sufficient for later professional practice. By stating, in our interviews, that they are still architects, and by self-identifying, for census purposes, as architects, they are making a clear statement that they are still within the architectural domain. But are not the men (who appear to de-register at the same rate, according to our indirect measurement of the situation) making the same statement? The answer must be in the affirmative; the men we interviewed were clearly engaged in architectural practice, from their own viewpoint, and they were unconcerned as to whether such practice was considered official or unofficial.

But the hypothesis of a parallel 'Continental' model encompasses the possibility that unregistered architects in general (both de-registered or never-registered) are engaged in *some* form of architectural practice and, as we know, there is a much higher proportion of women than of men in this category. As to the never-registered professional women, who merely differ from their de-registered sisters in that they have completed the educational but not professional qualifications, is it not possible that they, also, are participating in some form of 'unofficial' architectural practice? As we have indicated earlier, this appears likely but requires further exploration; what can be stated definitively on the basis of this research is that the experience of de-registered architects is consistent with the so-called Continental model, that is, that professional qualifications are serving as a sufficient basis for practice within a broadly defined professional domain. And we also know that Quebec women dominate this category of de-registered professionals in Canada. Could they be influenced by the French professional model in their choices? As we cited earlier (chapter 5, note 18), the gaining of professional qualifications is an important step, at least for certain of the Quebec de-registered professionals; thus, their rapid rate of entry to their association, followed by their rapid rate of exit, appears to be a means of asserting their autonomy from the professional association, thus providing the opportunity to carve out an alternative architectural career that fits their priorities.

Conclusion

As we come to the end of our study of Canadian women architects, we ponder the implications for other studies of professional women. First, we would like to signal to our researcher colleagues that the relegation of women to the 'marginalized' and 'ghettoized' sectors of a profession should not be taken for granted. As we have argued, the so-called women's specialities are not self-evident; in particular, in times of change and social turbulence, women are often called upon to play very different roles within their professions – and we should not be blinkered to their potential contributions. In effect, the delineation of the role of women within specific professions is an empirical issue, and should not be approached from the perspective that women occupy spaces men have designated for them.

For, to continue on the theme of the margins, who designates the spaces that are marginal to the professional project? Is it more 'central' to design monumental public projects or housing? Is it more important to undertake the nursing, nutritional, or surgical care of patients? Is it more important to educate the child or the young adult? Clearly, the answer to the initial question is that those specialities that are male-dominated are normatively viewed as central to the profession, whereas, in practice, the various professional contributions are interdependent. Thus, to speak of the 'margins' of the professions is to participate in a male discourse that merely serves to reinforce male dominance within the professional arena.

Such observations cause us to reflect more generally on an approach to the professions that would illuminate the participation of women in particular. Some thought should clearly be given to the heuristic value of the term 'professions.' If we think about women's work in general, is there a certain contribution in hiving off what, after all, is an elite and minority stratum of women's work? Does this add significantly to our understanding of women's workplace participation in general? Or is the very conception of the professions so profoundly masculinist that we enter into male priorities by using this term? The current study assumes that the concept has some importance for our understanding of women's work experience and, furthermore, that the segregation of the *male-dominated* professions from those in which women predominate reflects important experiential differences within the workplace. We note, however, that a recently published edited volume supports neither of these assumptions, virtually employing the term 'profession' as a synonym for 'occupation' (Smyth et al. 1999, 7) and certainly making little distinction between the male- and female-dominated professions. We believe that the question remains an open one and that we should accord considerable thought to the potential significance (or insignificance) of the term 'professions' for our conceptualization of women's work.

In opening up the discussion of the term, we also to need to confront what could be identified as the extant 'top-down' view of the professions with a 'bottom-up' view of the same workspace. Not only the traditional literature, but also much of the specific literature on gender and the professions, has assumed that the professions need to be theorized from an institutional rather than an experiential perspective. Certainly, traditional discussions of professional definitions and of professionalization, as well as recent feminist approaches to issues of professional closure, take the 'profession' as the main arena of discussion, as a result often homogenizing gendered experiences of such arenas. Empirical work has certainly opened up our understanding of these various experiences, which now need to be incorporated into our general conceptualization of the nature of the professions.

For, finally, in Acker's terms, we need to delineate in much greater detail the gendered substructure of the professions, together with the ongoing gendered processes (1992, 252ff.), and the way that this substructure is (or is not) being transformed by a significant proportion of 'non-gentlemanly' participation. Acker reminds us that organizational, and thus professional, practices, discourse, and ideologies are the ongoing means of reinforcing participants in their gendered spaces – not only physical, but also experiential. But women are not mere puppets to be acted upon and moved around the professional arena; as our study has clearly demonstrated, they are active agents in their own interests, refusing to be merely relegated to their gendered spaces, and actively seeking a redefinition of professional practice. It is this interaction between the existing gendered substructure and women's priorities and decisions that will give rise to the professional arenas of the future – and we need the research tools, both practical and conceptual, to be able to understand the changes.

Part of what we have learned from this study of women architects is that *no* existing categories of analysis concerning the professions should be taken for granted. In fact, it is extremely important to be enormously suspicious of *all* normatively accepted categories, for they are more than likely to hide important aspects of the gendered substructure. As Acker points out (1992, 258),

'The theory and practice of gender neutrality covers up, obscures, the underlying gender structure.' If we are to delineate the gendered processes that characterize the professional arena, we must liberate ourselves from research tools that obfuscate rather than illuminate the all-pervasive role of gender as it affects women's workplace experience.

For we join those who proclaim that 'women change the workplace' rather than those who consider that 'the workplace [will] change women.'[20] The only way that women can be viewed as *not* changing the workplace is if we insist on traditional perspectives for studies of their work. Obviously, if masculinist frameworks are the only ones available, it will be impossible to explore the wide-ranging parameters of change brought about by women. In effect, researchers themselves need to modify their vision and their perspective if they are to grasp the transformed workplace. We thank our women architects, both registered and de-registered, for allowing us to seize the changes that they are accomplishing within a key profession.

Appendix A:
Methodology

As indicated in the introduction, the approaches used in this research represent a combination of historical and sociological research methods. The resources used can be summarized under three main headings: (1) statistical sources; (2) archival sources; and (3) interview material.

Statistical Sources

Our statistical material is derived from three very different sources. First, we consulted all available census material on women architects from 1921 to 1991, and this provides the basis for several tabular presentations, particularly in chapter 2 and Appendix B. In collecting this material, we noted that the census definition of architects depends on an individual's (or relevant respondent's) responses to census questions about his or her recent work experience (chapter 2, note 5); we also noted that the census definition, in all the years covered except 1961, includes one or more specializations that would not be recognized by provincial architectural associations (chapter 2, note 6).

Vastly more time-consuming was our second approach to a statistical overview of the profession. Given that the architectural profession in Canada, at a national level, has maintained no complete statistical records for the period of our research, we were obliged to approach individual provincial associations[1] for data. We requested a 'package' of information from each provincial association that was to include comprehensive information on *every* woman who had ever been a member of the provincial association and aggregate data for current and former male members, by association status.[2] We recognized that

We are tremendously grateful to Sarah Baker and Jill Trower for the information they prepared for this appendix.

the preparation of such material would be a very time-consuming exercise for provincial associations; thus, we offered to pay staff or an individual, selected by the association, for the work involved, if this proved to be necessary. We remain enormously grateful to the provincial associations for their collaboration in this extensive data-collection exercise, which took place over a two-year period.

Finally, in order to complete the aggregate data on both women and men for the historical period covered, we used the directories of the Royal Architectural Institute of Canada, RAIC annual counts of provincial registrants, and/or provincial annual reports, most of which did not break down figures by gender. However, with our complete listing of all women who had ever registered with provincial associations, we were able to derive totals for male members and calculate proportions, by gender, over the research period.

Archival Sources

In order to uncover women involved in the work of architecture and women-designed buildings, more than 160 requests for information were dispatched to various individuals and associations. Provincial associations, the RAIC, Canadian schools of architecture, individual scholars and architects, and more than 70 archives were asked to contribute materials. The responses were numerous, and were mostly significant in revealing how very little documentation on women's architectural work can be found across Canada.

In the beginning, two standard sources were used (optimistically) to gather published documentation on projects by women and by firms where women were employed. The *Canadian Architectural Periodical Index* covered the period from 1940 to 1980, and the *Avery Index to Art and Architecture Periodicals* covered the later period. In order to construct a portrait of the profession that women have sought to enter over time, a survey of the entire run (from 1924 to 1973) of *The Journal, Royal Architectural Institute of Canada* was carried out. Other architectural journals, such as *Canadian Architect*, were also surveyed.

Less comprehensive surveys of *Chatelaine, Saturday Night, Maclean's,* and *Canadian Homes and Gardens* also helped to reveal the popular images of women and the profession of architecture. Although many articles featured the careers of relatively well-known women architects, others documented the work of lesser-known, or even anonymous, Canadian women. We also explored all available archival sources, as well as contacting individual women architects in our search for historical material. We posted notices in newsletters, and many women architects responded. As a result, we have compiled extensive biographical files on hundreds of women who have studied and practised architecture in Canada.

Interviews

A significant proportion of the time of the research team was devoted to interviews with two groups of architects: (1) women architects who had registered with the Ontario and Quebec provincial associations prior to 1970 ('registered architects'); and (2) former members of provincial associations in Ontario, Quebec, and the Western provinces over the total research period ('de-registered architects').

Registered Architects

Interviews with registered architects were confined to Ontario and Quebec in the pre-1970 period for two main reasons. First, and not surprisingly, these two provinces dominate the total of women registrants in Canada for, as can be calculated from figures provided in table B.7 in Appendix B, 79 per cent of all women registrants over the research period were members of these two provincial associations. Second, the forty-eight women members who registered in the two provinces prior to 1970 constituted a 'manageable' population for a program that aimed to interview as many of these still-living pioneer members as possible. In practice, we interviewed twelve (of eighteen) members from Quebec, and nineteen (of thirty) members from Ontario. Of the six remaining Quebec members, one was well-documented in a thesis, two had died, two could not be contacted despite multiple attempts to do so, and one refused to participate in our project. Five Ontario women were deceased by the time of our study, and two refused to participate. Many of the Ontario women, we felt, were well-documented in the exhibition put together by the University of Toronto. Since we were able to use this material, in some cases interviews were considered unnecessary.

These interviews with women registrants were not rigidly structured. The education, family background, work experience, family composition, and family duties of the women were established, and the women were encouraged to comment on influences on their career choices, and their university and work experiences. The interviews were taped, and careful notes were taken. In addition, we gathered *curricula vitarum* and any other available written material concerning the interview subjects and their architectural projects, including newspaper articles that commented on these early women architects, and biographical information from secondary sources to supplement interview mate-

TABLE A.1
De-registered women interviewed (Quebec men in parentheses), by province and decade of registration

	BC	AB	SK	MB	ON	QC	QC(M)	Total	TBI*
To 1950s			1	1	2	1		5	4.0
1960s		1			1	1		3	3.5
1970s						4	(2)	4	7.1
Subtotal 1950s to 1970s								12	14.6
1980s	1				1	9	(4)	11	11.7
1990s						4	(4)	4	2.2
Subtotal 1980s and 1990s								15	13.9
TOTAL	1	1	1	1	4	19	(10)	27	28.5
TBI*	2.5	2.6	0.9	1.1	5.4	16			28.5

*Indicates desirable numbers to be interviewed according to proportions by province and decade of registration

rial. Women-designed projects in the Montreal, Ottawa, and Toronto areas were photographed. Matrices synthesizing all the material on registered architects were prepared.

De-registered Architects

In the case of the de-registered women architects, our goal was to interview a sample of thirty women, in proportion to both the distribution of de-registered women across the country and throughout the time period of the project. In practice, a negligible proportion of de-registered women came from the Atlantic provinces (9 women, or a mere 4 per cent, over the seventy-two-year period of the research, cf. table 2.4), of whom not one could be contacted; thus, in practice the sample includes women from Quebec to the West Coast. In addition, we interviewed a small sample of de-registered men, from Quebec only, in an attempt to grasp gender differences.

It should be underlined that the challenge for this set of interviews arose from the difficulty in contacting individuals who had resigned from provincial associations as early as the 1940s or 1950s, and for whom, on occasion, we had points of contact from provincial associations that were considerably out of date. We used all possible additional sources – university alumni associations, telephone directories for major Canadian cities, and a snowball method based on the women we were able to contact. With all these attempts, it was possible to conduct twenty-seven interviews with women, and ten with men, over the research period. Table A.1 provides the relevant breakdown.

As can be seen, despite the difficulties in contacting subjects, the numbers of women hover around the desirable level and should not invalidate a general image of de-registrants over the past fifty years from Quebec to the West Coast; the small group of men provide some contrasting material for the Quebec women.

Interviews started with the completion of a brief questionnaire covering the subject's educational background (dates, degree, discipline, university); work experience (position, firm, dates); years of membership in any provincial association; father's and mother's occupations; and household characteristics during the working career (number of persons, relationship to the subject). The material collected in this way was used as a basis for the open-ended interviews that followed and that ranged widely around the subject's reasons for de-registering from a provincial association. Interviews, which were recorded, lasted from ninety minutes to two hours; they were later transcribed verbatim and analysed with the assistance of the computer analysis program, *The Ethnograph (4.0).*

Appendix B:
Additional Tables

Note: The census uses 'random rounding' to multiples of 5, particularly since 1971; this may affect percentages and totals.

TABLE B.1
Dentists, showing percentages of women for Canada and the provinces, 1961–1991[a]

	1961 N = 5,469	1971 N = 6,425	1981 N = 10,290	1986 N = 12,075	1991 N = 12,825
Canada	4.2	4.8	7.8	13.3	15.4
British Columbia	3.3	3.5	5.3	9.1	10.5
Alberta	5.4	4.3	5.9	7.6	13.1
Saskatchewan	4.5	2.6	6.3	18.6	15.1
Manitoba	2.8	4.1	–	12.6	10.9
Ontario	*5.3*	*6.0*	*7.4*	*13.5*	*16.3*
Quebec	*2.5*	*4.4*	*10.4*	*18.0*	*19.4*
New Brunswick	3.7	–	3.0	6.8	6.8
Nova Scotia	8.9	3.0	24.0	11.8	19.7
Prince Edward Island	–	–	–	–	–
Newfoundland	7.1	7.1	9.5	18.2	11.5

[a]Census of Canada: 1961, 3.1, Table 6; 1971, Cat. 94-717, Table 2; 1981, Cat. 92-920, Table 1; 1986 and 1991, Cat. 93-327, Table 1

TABLE B.2
Engineers, showing percentages of women for Canada and the provinces, 1961–1991[a]

	1961 N = 43,066	1971 N = 76,885	1981 N = 119,490	1986 N = 127,565	1991 N = 159,380
Canada	0.3	1.6	3.6	5.5	8.8
British Columbia	0.1	1.4	2.5	4.4	4.8
Alberta	0.1	1.4	4.1	5.6	6.9
Saskatchewan	0.2	0.3	2.4	3.9	3.5
Manitoba	–	0.9	2.8	5.5	7.1
Ontario	*0.3*	*1.8*	*3.6*	*5.5*	*9.7*
Quebec	*0.4*	*1.7*	*4.2*	*6.7*	*11.7*
New Brunswick	0.4	0.8	3.3	4.2	4.9
Nova Scotia	0.1	1.2	4.2	4.4	7.0
Prince Edward Island	–	–	6.3	7.1	18.0
Newfoundland	–	0.6	2.0	3.3	5.2

[a]Census of Canada: 1961, 3.1, Table 6; 1971, Cat. 94-717, Table 2; 1981, Cat. 92-920, Table 1; 1986 and 1991, Cat. 93-327, Table 1

TABLE B.3
Lawyers, showing percentages of women for Canada and the provinces, 1961–1991[a]

	1961 N = 12,008	1971 N = 16,315	1981 N = 34,200	1986 N = 41,980	1991 N = 53,570
Canada	2.6	4.7	15.1	21.8	29.1
British Columbia	3.5	4.9	17.4	21.0	31.7
Alberta	1.7	4.0	14.9	23.6	24.4
Saskatchewan	2.0	5.9	18.1	21.7	26.0
Manitoba	1.5	2.2	13.1	17.1	22.2
Ontario	*3.3*	*5.0*	*12.7*	*19.8*	*27.6*
Quebec	*1.8*	*5.0*	*18.3*	*25.3*	*34.0*
New Brunswick	2.3	3.0	11.5	16.0	22.8
Nova Scotia	1.7	3.8	13.6	24.9	26.2
Prince Edward Island	–	–	18.8	29.0	18.5
Newfoundland	1.4	5.2	9.3	13.7	16.5

[a]Census of Canada: 1961, 3.1, Table 6; 1971, Cat. 94-717, Table 2; 1981, Cat. 92-920, Table 1; 1986 and 1991, Cat. 93-327, Table 1

TABLE B.4
Physicians, showing percentages of women for Canada and the provinces, 1961–1991[a]

	1961 $N = 21{,}290$	1971 $N = 28{,}580$	1981 $N = 40{,}545$	1986 $N = 46{,}800$	1991 $N = 54{,}515$
Canada	6.8	10.1	17.1	21.1	26.7
British Columbia	7.4	10.3	15.4	18.4	24.2
Alberta	7.7	11.2	13.7	19.4	23.7
Saskatchewan	6.9	9.0	19.3	18.8	22.3
Manitoba	6.6	10.3	14.2	17.8	26.8
Ontario	*7.8*	*10.6*	*18.2*	*22.2*	*26.9*
Quebec	*5.7*	*9.7*	*18.4*	*23.3*	*29.1*
New Brunswick	4.6	2.8	9.5	17.8	18.6
Nova Scotia	4.6	9.0	14.2	19.3	30.7
Prince Edward Island	4.3	6.2	12.9	10.5	17.6
Newfoundland	5.0	9.9	15.9	11.4	22.6

[a]Census of Canada: 1961, 3.1, Table 6; 1971, Cat. 94-717, Table 2; 1981, Cat. 92-920, Table 1; 1986 and 1991, Cat. 93-327, Table 1

TABLE B.5
Women registrants in the AIBC, by place of birth and decade
of entry, 1930–1992[a]

	Canadian-born registrants	Non-Canadian-born registrants[b]
1930–9	0	1 100%
1940–9	1 25%	3 75%
1950–9	2 67%	1 33%
1960–9	0	5 100%
Total pre-1970	3 23%	10 77%
1970–9	5 26%	14 74%
1980–9	29 71%	12 29%
1990–2	26 79%	7 21%
Total 1970–92	60 65%	33 35%
TOTAL	63 59%	43 40%

[a]Data prepared for the 'Designing Women' project from registration records of the AIBC. There is one registrant for whom
information is not available, making a total of 107 registrants
over this period.
[b]Of 43 born abroad, significant numbers came from Great
Britain (10), the United States (6), Czechoslovakia (4), and
Poland (4).

TABLE B.6
Women registrants in the AIBC, by place of education and decade
of entry, 1930–1992[a]

	Canadian-educated registrants	Non-Canadian-educated registrants[b]
1930–9	0	1 100%
1940–9	2 50%	2 50%
1950–9	2 67%	1 33%
1960–9	2 40%	3 60%
Total pre-1970	6 46%	7 54%
1970–9	8 42%	11 58%
1980–9	33 79%	9 21%
1990–2	27 82%	6 18%
Total 1970–92	68 72%	26 28%
TOTAL	74 69%	33 21%

[a]Data prepared for the 'Designing Women' project from registration records of the AIBC.
[b]Of 33 educated abroad, significant groups were educated in the
United States (12), Great Britain (8), Poland (4), and Czechoslovakia (3).

TABLE B.7
Women entrants to provincial associations, by province and decade of registration, 1920–1992[a]

	BC		AB		SK		MB		ON		QC		NB		NS		PE		NF		Total	
	T	F %	T	F %	T	F %	T	F %	T	F %	T	F %	T	F %	T	F %	T	F %	T	F %	T	F %
1920–9	125	–	1	1 / 100	–		–		158	–	1	–	–		–		–		–		285	1 / 0.4
1930–9	26	1 / 3.8	4	1 / 25.0	1	–	–		354	2 / 0.6	17	–	13	–	–		–		–		415	4 / 1.0
1940–9	64	4 / 6.3	8	5 / 62.5	1	–	7	2 / 28.6	184	5 / 2.7	126	3 / 2.4	4	–	2	–	–		–		396	19 / 4.8
1950–9	214	3 / 1.4	56	3 / 5.4	19	2 / 10.5	35	1 / 2.9	588	8 / 1.4	296	5 / 1.7	21	–	4	–	–		16	–	1,249	22 / 1.8
1960–9	235	5 / 2.1	48	2 / 4.2	19	1 / 5.3	40	3 / 7.5	660	15 / 2.3	410	10 / 2.4	23	–	25	2 / 8.0	–		5	–	1,465	38 / 2.6
1970–9	450	19 / 4.2	206	12 / 5.8	26	–	58	3 / 5.2	913	46 / 5.0	1,025	76 / 7.4	33	2 / 6.1	55	2 / 3.6	11	1 / 9.1	7	–	2,784	161 / 5.8
1980–9	462	42 / 9.1	232	22 / 9.5	46	6 / 13.0	107	10 / 9.3	1,199	132 / 11.0	1,230	313 / 25.4	44	4 / 9.1	80	11 / 13.8	5	1 / 20.0	29	–	3,434	541 / 15.8
1990–2	253	33 / 13.0	107	12 / 11.2	18	–	42	5 / 11.9	432	69 / 16.0	403	149 / 37.0	30	2 / 6.7	5	1 / 20.0	2	–	3	–	1,295	271 / 20.9
1920–92	1,829	107 / 5.9	662	58 / 8.6	130	9 / 6.9	289	24 / 8.3	4,488	277 / 6.2	3,508	556 / 15.8	168	8 / 4.7	171	16 / 9.0	18	2 / 11.1	60	–	11,323	1,057 / 9.3
1960–92																					8,978	1,011 / 11.3

[a]Data prepared for the 'Designing Women' project from registration records of the Architectural Institute of British Columbia (AIBC), Alberta Association of Architects (AAA), Saskatchewan Association of Architects (SAA), Manitoba Association of Architects (MAA), Ontario Association of Architects (OAA), Ordre des architectes du Québec (OAQ), Architects' Association of New Brunswick (AANB), Nova Scotia Association of Architects (NSAA), Architects Association of Prince Edward Island (AAPEI), and the Newfoundl and Association of Architects (NAA). There are 17 registrants for whom full information is not available; they are omitted from this table.

TABLE B.8

All registered architects, and the percentage of women architects, by provincial association, 1961–1992[a]

	BC			AB			SK			MB			ON			QC			NB			NS			PE			NF			Canada		
	T	F	%	T	F	%	T	F	%	T	F	%	T	F	%	T	F	%	T	F	%	T	F	%	T	F	%	T	F	%	T	F	%
1961	251	3	1.2	157	6	3.8	58	1	1.7	148	1	0.7	982	11	1.1	692	6	0.9	26	–	–	52	–	–	–	–	–	16	–	–	2,382	28	1.2
1971	417	6	1.4	227	8	3.5	72	–	–	204	1	0.5	1,356	25	1.8	829	19	2.3	41	1	2.4	81	2	2.5	–	–	–	19	–	–	3,246	62	1.9
1981	573	27	4.7	501	20	4.0	79	1	1.3	127	3	2.4	1,892	68	3.6	1,643	119	7.2	39	–	–	105	6	5.7	10	1	10.0	27	–	–	4,996	245	4.9
1986	936	48	5.1	546	30	5.5	128	5	3.9	255	10	3.9	2,177	121	5.6	2,090	240	11.5	68	–	–	175	11	6.3	19	–	–	39	–	–	6,433	465	7.2
1991	1,052	76	7.2	585	40	6.8	133	4	3.0	328	15	4.6	2,511	216	8.7	2,623	435	16.6	93	3	3.2	188	13	6.9	16	–	–	38	–	–	7,567	802	10.6
1992	1,091	87	8.0	576	35	6.1	97	3	3.1	303	15	5.0	2,489	228	9.2	2,595	472	18.2	91	5	5.5	178	12	6.7	16	–	–	38	–	–	7,472	857	11.5

[a] Data prepared for the 'Designing Women' project from registration records of the AIBC, AAA, SAA, MAA, OAA, OAQ, AANB, NSAA, AAPEI, and NAA.

TABLE B.9
Women architects as a percentage of total architects, by province and census year, 1921–1991[a]

	BC	AB	SK	MB	ON	QC	NB	NS	PE	NF	Canada
1921 (N=)[c]	D[b]	D	D	D	D	D	D	D	D	D	0.3% (1,169)
1931 (N=)	D	D	D	D	D	D	D	D	D	D	0.2% (1,298)
1941 (N=)	2.8% (107)	6.5% (31)	–	5.0% (40)	1.6% (515)	0.2% (448)	– (13)	–	–	–	1.2% (1,313)
1951 (N=)	2.2% (139)	4.0% (100)	13.8% (29)	1.2% (86)	2.8% (744)	1.5% (581)	4.5% (22)	–	(1)	(9)	2.5% (1,740)
1961 (N=)	2.2% (321)	3.0% (197)	1.4% (73)	1.6% (183)	1.8% (1,138)	2.9% (921)	– (34)	2.0% (50)	(6)	(17)	2.2% (2,940)
1971 (N=)	2.7% (555)	1.7% (300)	4.8% (105)	2.9% (170)	2.3% (1,500)	4.2% (1,185)	– (50)	7.1% (140)	(10)	(25)	3.0% (4,040)
1981 (N=)	8.2% (1,225)	8.8% (850)	–	4.3% (235)	5.0% (2,240)	9.7% (2,065)	9.5% (105)	4.8% (210)	(20)	(45)	7.3% (7,110)
1986 (N=)	7.9% (1,270)	8.4% (655)	8.7% (115)	10.4% (240)	10.9% (3,130)	18.2% (2,720)	23.8% (105)	17.1% (205)	(15)	(45)	12.7% (8,580)
1991 (N=)	11.6% (1,805)	18.8% (850)	11.8% (85)	9.8% (205)	17.9% (4,365)	25.0% (4,025)	11.8% (85)	13.0% (270)	(25)	(65)	19.1% (11,810)

[a]Census of Canada: 1921 & 1931 data from the 1941 Census Trend Report (Cat. 98-194-M33); 1941, 1951, 1961 data from the 1961 Census Trend Report (Cat. 98-551-LS-1); 1971 & 1981 data from the 1986 Trend Report (Cat. 93-151); 1986 & 1991 data from the 1991 census (Cat. 93-327)

[b]D = Data not available for these dates

[c]N = Total number of architects in province or in Canada

TABLE B.10
Architects by sex, showing age groups, for Canada, 1991[a]

	Total	Age group										
		15–19 years	20–4 years	25–9 years	30–4 years	35–9 years	40–4 years	45–9 years	50–4 years	55–9 years	60–4 years	65+ years
Male	9,855	–	210	1,340	1,595	1,830	1,595	1,150	790	550	415	380
	100%		2%	14%	16%	19%	16%	12%	8%	6%	4%	4%
Female	2,355	–	115	725	685	445	205	70	60	15	10	25
	100%		5%	31%	29%	19%	9%	3%	3%	1%	0%	1%

[a]Based on the 1991 census custom tabulation provided by Statistics Canada.

TABLE B.11
Architects by sex, showing highest level of schooling, for Canada, 1991[a]

| | Total | Highest level of schooling | | | | |
		Elementary & secondary only	Other non-university	Some university without certificate	University[b] with certificate	University degree[c]
Male	9,850	325	1,305	185	520	7,515
	100%	3%	13%	2%	5%	76%
Female	2,360	45	230	20	125	1,940
	100%	2%	10%	1%	5%	82%

[a]Based on the 1991 census custom tabulation provided by Statistics Canada.
[b]Below Bachelor level.
[c]Includes university with degree; university with BA or professional degree; university certificate above BA; university with Master's degree; university with doctorate.

TABLE B.12
Architects by sex, showing labour-force activity and weeks worked in 1990, total and mostly full-time, for Canada, 1991[a]

| | In the labour force[b] | | | Worked in 1990 | | | | | | | |
| | | | | Total | | 1–26 weeks | | 27–48 weeks | | 49–52 weeks | |
	Total in labour force	Employed	Unemployed	Total	Mostly full-time	Total	Mostly full-time	Total	Mostly full-time	Total	Mostly full-time
Male (N = 9,860)	9,555 100%	8,950 94%	600 6%	9,860 100%	9,395 95%	920	760 8%	1,590	1,455 15%	7,275	7,180 76%
Female (N = 2,350)	2,260 100%	2,000 88%	255 11%	2,350 100%	2,130 91%	425	370 17%	515	445 21%	1,370	1,315 62%

[a]Based on the 1991 census custom tabulation provided by Statistics Canada.
[b]This category is also referred to as the 'experienced labour force.'

TABLE B.13
Architects by sex, showing class of worker, for
Canada, 1991[a]

	Class of worker		
	Salaried workers[b]	Self-employed[c]	Total
Male	11,515	2,050	13,565
	85%	15%	100%
Female	2,475	280	2,755
	90%	10%	100%

[a]Based on the 1991 census custom tabulation provided by
Statistics Canada.
[b]Includes employees, paid workers, and self-employed in
incorporated companies.
[c]Includes self-employed in unincorporated companies.

TABLE B.14
Architects by sex, showing ethnic origins, for Canada, 1991[a]

	Single Origin										Multiple Origins			
	Total	Canadian	British	French	German	Italian	Ukrainian	Dutch	Native peoples	Other	British & French	British & other	French & other	Other
Male	9,790	155	1,570	2,130	240	325	200	130	10	2,415	285	1,620	205	505
	100%	2%	16%	22%	2%	3%	2%	1%	0%	25%	3%	17%	2%	5%
Female	2,335	40	190	655	60	35	20	10	0	645	105	310	60	205
	100%	2%	8%	28%	3%	2%	1%	0%		28%	5%	13%	3%	9%

aBased on the 1991 census custom tabulation provided by Statistics Canada.

TABLE B.15
Architects by sex, showing mother tongue, for Canada,
1991[a]

	Total	Mother tongue		
		English	French	Other
Male	9,775	4,760	2,440	2,575
	100%	49%	25%	26%
Female	2,325	940	810	575
	100%	40%	35%	25%

[a]Based on the 1991 census custom tabulation provided
by Statistics Canada.

TABLE B.16
Architects by sex, showing marital status by age group, for Canada, 1991[a]

		Single				Married[b]					Separated	Widowed	Divorced
	Total	Total	15–24 years	25–44 years	45–64 years	Total	15–24 years	25–44 years	45–64 years	65+ years	Total	Total	Total
Male	9,825	1,815 18%	160	1,485	170	7,430 76%	45	4,570	2,460	355	180 2%	55 1%	345 4%
Female	2,345	800 34%	85	705	10	1,470 63%	30	1,290	125	25	25 1%	15 1%	35 1%

[a]Based on the 1991 census custom tabulation provided by Statistics Canada.
[b]Includes common-law marriages.

TABLE B.17
Architects by sex, showing place of birth, for Canada, 1991[a]

					Place of birth			
					Outside Canada[b]			
						Europe		
	Total	Canada	Total[c]	USA	Total[e]	United Kingdom	Other Europe	Other[d]
Male	9,850	6,295	3,555	215	1,920	615	1,305	1,420
	100%	64%	36%	2%	19%	6%	13%	14%
Female	2,355	1,640	715	70	355	45	310	290
	100%	70%	30%	3%	15%	2%	13%	12%

[a]Based on the 1991 census custom tabulation provided by Statistics Canada.
[b]Includes persons born outside Canada who are Canadian citizens by birth.
[c]Includes all other birthplaces outside Canada.
[d]Other comprises: Central & South America, Caribbean & Bermuda, Africa, India, Other Asia Oceania, and Other.
[e]Includes all Europe.

TABLE B.18
Architects by sex, showing period of immigration, for Canada, 1991[a]

			Period of immigration		
	Before 1961	1961–70	1971–80	1981–91	Total outside Canada
Male	785	860	1,000	835	3,480
	23%	25%	29%	24%	100%
Female	75	115	155	330	675
	11%	17%	23%	49%	100%

[a]Based on the 1991 census custom tabulation provided by Statistics Canada.

TABLE B.19
Women registered and leaving the OAA, by decade of entry, 1930–1992[a]

	No. women registrants	No./% women exiting[b]	No./% women mobile[b]	No./% women retiring[b]	No./% women deceased[b]	Total No./% women leaving[b]
1930–9	2	1 _50.0_	0	1 _50.0_	0	2 _100.0_
1940–9	5	1 _20.0_	1 _20.0_	3 _60.0_	0	5 _100.0_
1950–9	8	3 _37.5_	1 _12.5_	1 _12.5_	0	5 _62.5_
Pre-1960 total	15	5 _33.3_	2 _13.3_	5 _33.3_	0	12 _80.0_
1960–9	15	3 _20.0_	1 _6.7_	4 _26.7_	0	8 _53.3_
1970–9	46	5 _10.9_	7 _15.2_	1 _2.2_	3 _6.5_	16 _34.8_
Total 1960–79	61	8 _13.1_	8 _13.1_	5 _8.2_	3 _4.9_	24 _39.3_
1980–9	132	6 _4.5_	2 _1.5_	0	0	8 _6.1_
1990–2	69	4 _5.8_	2 _2.9_	0	0	6 _8.7_
TOTAL	277	23 _8.3_	14 _5.1_	10 _3.6_	3 _1.1_	50 _18.1_

[a]Data prepared for the 'Designing Women' project from registration records of the OAA.
[b]See table 2.4 for a definition of these terms.

TABLE B.20
Women registered and leaving the OAQ, by decade of entry, 1940–1992[a]

	No. women registrants	No./% women exiting[b]	No./% women mobile[b]	No./% women retiring[b]	No./% women deceased[b]	Total No./% women leaving[b]
1940–9	3	1 / *33.3*	0	0	1 / *33.3*	2 / *66.7*
1950–9	5	2 / *40.0*	0	2 / *40.0*	0	4 / *80.0*
Pre-1960 total	8	3 / *37.5*	0	2 / *25.0*	1 / *12.5*	6 / *75.0*
1960–9	10	5 / *50.0*	1 / *10.0*	1 / *10.0*	0	7 / *70.0*
1970–9	76	18 / *23.7*	5 / *6.6*	1 / *1.3*	1 / *1.3*	25 / *32.9*
Total 1960–79	86	23 / *26.7*	6 / *7.0*	2 / *2.3*	1 / *1.2*	32 / *37.2*
1980–9	313	36 / *11.5*	2 / *0.6*	0	0	38 / *12.1*
1990–2	149	5 / *3.4*	1 / *0.7*	0	1 / *0.7*	7 / *4.7*
TOTAL	556	67 / *12.1*	9 / *1.6*	4 / *0.7*	3 / *0.5*	83 / *14.9*

[a]Data prepared for the 'Designing Women' project from registration records of the OAQ; no women entered prior to 1942.
[b]See table 2.4 for a definition of these terms.

Appendix C:
Lexicon

Architects: All those listed by the census as architects (including architects and building architects in all years; plus naval, marine, and landscape architects in all years except 1961)

De-registered Architects: All those who have been members of a provincial association, but who have discontinued their membership for reasons other than mobility to another provincial association, retirement, or death (cf: 'Exiting' below)

'Exiting from an architectural association':   Discontinuing membership in a provincial association by:

a. resigning and not re-registering in another provincial association;
b. moving to a status which does not permit calling oneself 'architect' (e.g., associate status in some provinces) and not re-registering in another provincial association;
c. retiring 'early,' that is, prior to thirty years of practice or prior to retirement age

'Leaving an architectural association':   Includes all those who exit, plus:

a. those who move to another provincial association after resigning or taking non-architect status;
b. those who retire after at least thirty years of practice or prior to retirement age;
c. those who die during the career period of thirty years

Never-Registered Architects: All university graduates in architecture who have never registered with provincial associations

Registered Architects: All 'architects' and 'building architects' who have registered with provincial associations

Unregistered Architects: All architects (as defined above) who have not registered with provincial associations

Notes

1: Introduction

1 On U.S. women architects, see Anderson 1980, Berkeley 1989, Cole 1973, Hayden 1981, Torre 1977, and Wright 1977; on British women architects, see Adams 1996b, 160–2, and Walker 1984, 1989.

2 On Hill's career, see van Ginkel 1993, 16, and Contreras, Ferrara, and Karpinski 1993, 18–20. Although Hill was the first registered woman architect in Canada, there is evidence that women may have designed major buildings here as early as the 1840s. On the career of Ethel Charles, see Walker 1989, 99–100. For a discussion of the acceptance of women to the Royal Institute of British Architects, see 'The Admission of Lady Associates.' On Bethune, see Stern 1959, 66.

3 Anthony kindly provided us with information on her forthcoming book; a description and excerpts from her interviews are available on her Web site, *http://www2.arch.uiuc.edu/kanthony/diversity.html*; the project is mentioned in several articles in the professional press, including Dixon 1994, 61.

4 A partial list of these is included in Greer 1982, 41.

5 Since Willis spent time at McGill in 1996 as a Visiting Scholar, she was able to include some comparisons with our project in her dissertation.

6 We are limiting discussion to the so-called male-dominated professions, where at least 65 per cent (Marshall 1989) to 70 per cent (Jacobs 1989) of professionals are male, on the assumption that the 'female-dominated' professions (e.g., nursing, social work, teaching) pose very different issues. While the theoretical work covers a wide range of male-dominated professions, the empirical work examined will be limited in practice to professions that may be considered parallel to architecture.

7 We are using census data in this instance (see tables B.1–B.4 in Appendix B); the various advantages of census and other material are discussed in detail in chapter 2.

8 There is a surprisingly limited literature on the subject of the contemporary situation of women in the male-dominated professions in Canada. The work by Hagan and Kay (1995) on women lawyers is the only book-length study of this topic of which we are aware. A doctoral thesis on women in dentistry (Adams 1997) covers the period up to 1917. A recent edited work (Smyth et al. 1999) purports to cover the professions, though the main thrust is a focus on women's work in general; certain male-dominated 'professions' (medicine, forestry, accountancy, and academia) are included, on occasion from a biographical or group-biographical perspective. The engineering profession has started to attract attention (Schirmer and Tancred 1996) but some of the work covers very limited topics (e.g., Carrier 1995). Admittedly, there are historical studies of women in medicine (Mitchinson 1991) and comparative studies on women in various professions (e.g., medicine and law: Kinnear 1995), but these do not cover the contemporary situation. There are several studies of women in the female-dominated professions, including pharmacy, which has recently been 'feminized' in Canada, but for reasons already indicated we are omitting the female-dominated professions. We do not include studies of professional women outside Canada (other than architects) for the very good reason that comparisons with professions that are both very different *and* located in a different cultural context begin to be tenuous.

9 Sarfatti Larson, in her wide-ranging study of U.S. architecture, would agree on this point; architecture, she writes, has artistic, technical, and social dimensions (1993, 4).

10 Chaplin's student work, however, was published in *RAIC Journal* 21/4 (April 1944): 74.

11 Please see the lexicon (Appendix C) for a definition of this term and various other new terms that we use to refer to women (and men) architects.

12 We use the term 'Modernism' in a general sense to refer to the undecorated buildings, with a frank expression of structure, following the work of Le Corbusier and the so-called International Style architects.

2: Entering Male-Dominated Practice, 1920–1992

1 The Royal Architectural Institute of Canada (RAIC) has attempted, however, at various points over the years, to coordinate such data, albeit in an incomplete fashion. Please see the next section of this chapter for a fuller discussion of the responsibilities of the RAIC and provincial associations.

2 We are most grateful to the provincial associations for their collaboration in this undertaking, which was a careful – and painful – process extending over a two-year period.

3 The fee varies from one province to another, but is generally in the range of $550–$750 per annum; professional liability insurance has become obligatory in recent

years for those who practise, in the initial years of membership costing around $500–$550 per year.

4 This and other similar terms are defined in the lexicon.

5 The pertinent Census questions are number 39: 'What kind of work was this person doing [last week or during the most recent job of longest duration]?' and number 40: 'In this work, what were this person's most important duties or activities?' (Statistics Canada 1997).

6 It should be noted that the census definition (in all census years covered in this research, except 1961) includes one or more of the following architectural 'specializations,' which are not recognized by the provincial associations: landscape, marine, and naval architecture. It is only in 1961 that the professional and census definitions cover identical work, that is, architecture and building architecture; this identity of coverage will prove useful in a discussion later in the chapter. Provincial associations check very carefully on the type of education and previous experience prior to the admission of a member.

7 The exact dates of foundation of these provincial associations are as follows: Ontario 1889; Quebec 1890; Alberta 1906; Saskatchewan 1911; Manitoba 1914; British Columbia 1914; Nova Scotia 1932; New Brunswick 1933; Newfoundland 1949; and Prince Edward Island 1972 (Clark 1988: figure 2).

8 The information on these three early registrants is drawn from Clark 1988, 4; van Ginkel 1993, 15ff.; Contreras, Ferrara, and Karpinski 1993, 18–20; and Simmins 1989, 104ff.

9 This refers to our research interviews, providing the gender of the respondent and the interview number.

10 It is well known in architectural history that Vancouver in particular was more accepting of Modernism. Its acceptance of women practitioners seems part of the same willingness to do things differently (see Liscombe 1997).

11 Taken from University of Manitoba Faculty of Architecture list of members of the department, school, and faculty from 1915 to 1966, based on the data of university calendar inclusion and deletion. The list was compiled by Jim Siemens, 2 March 1996. We are extremely grateful to Jill Trower for bringing this information to our attention.

12 See Ahrentzen and Groat 1992.

13 For a more qualitative approach to this issue, see chapter 4.

14 Britain, the United States, Czechoslovakia, and Poland dominate as both the birthplaces and the countries of education of these immigrant women.

15 Similar data for Quebec are presented in chapter 4.

16 As compared, for example, to the engineering profession, which had about 160,000 *members* as of the early 1990s (Canadian Council of Professional Engineers 1994–5).

17 We are pleased to note that our Laval colleagues Carole Després and Denise Piché are leading a research team that will study Quebec women architects in much greater detail, though we are not aware of a comparative study for an anglophone province.

18 Project data show that the average age on entry to provincial associations is about thirty.

19 As table B.9 in Appendix B indicates, the census records no data by province before 1941.

20 At first glance, this result appears to contradict Caven's recent research on women architects in the Nottingham area in England. She argues that, for the thirty-seven women she interviewed, the most common form of employment (for seventeen of them) was 'self-employment'; the definition is a broad one, including principals of a practice, those working on contract, as well as sole practitioners (1998, 9). However, she does acknowledge later that the numbers for male practitioners would be comparable (p. 14).

21 The men are also drawn from Asia (between 1 per cent and 9 per cent) and the United States (5 per cent).

22 Calculated on the basis of the difference between census and association totals (4,243) as a percentage of the census total. Blau (1984, 16) also documents (for the United States) that architecture, in comparison with other professions, ranks low with respect to the percentage of practitioners who are licensed. We should also note that there are three provinces (Saskatchewan, Manitoba, and to a minor extent New Brunswick) where the provincial association figures *exceed* those recorded by the census. We have no explanation for these anomalies except to suggest that a number of architects are maintaining registration in these provinces while working elsewhere; but why these particular provinces?

23 Feldman (1989) supports this statement; however, there is no documentation as to the extent of the difference as we are able to provide here.

24 These percentages are calculated by deriving the number of registered women professionals in 1991 (10.6 per cent of 7,567 = 802) and subtracting this number from the total number of women who describe their work as that of an architect (19.1 per cent of 11,810 = 2,256) to give 1,454. This latter figure is then calculated as a proportion of all women who declare themselves (or are described as) architects, that is, 64 per cent. Similar calculations can be made for men (29 per cent) and for women and men together (36 per cent).

25 Obviously, other hypotheses are possible, but appear to us improbable. For example, the higher proportion of unregistered women professionals *could* be attributable to the greater propensity of women (rather than men) without appropriate qualifications to describe their work as that of an architect. There seems to be no intrinsic reason why women and men should differ on this dimension.

26 However, we are pleased to note that the Després/Piché study 1993, A11, already cited, proposes to accomplish this task for Quebec 'depuis l'entrée significative des femmes dans la profession' ('since the significant entry of women to the profession'), and should eventually provide us with relevant data, at least for one province.

27 Our records show that in fact only seven women graduates of Ontario universities (specifically the University of Toronto) registered in *any* provincial association during this period (see table 2.2). If Clark's estimate of the total number of graduates is correct, and even if we include the two registrants whose university of origin is not known, a maximum of one-third of Ontario women graduates registered during this period.

28 See the lexicon for a definition of this term. It should be noted that, when we are talking about the national presence of registered women architects, mobility from one provincial association to another is obviously not pertinent as a means of 'leaving' the profession.

29 This result would be supported by Rosin and Korabik (1992), who underline that one of the 'myths' of the workplace is that more women than men managers are leaving organizations. They maintain that poor research methodology has resulted in such knowledge, based more on fiction than on fact.

30 It should be noted that Mary Clark estimates that the rate, up to 1960, was about 25 per cent, though she includes 'marriage, death or other social obligations' as among the principal reasons for such departures (1988, 6). Her tentative pre-1960 estimate is not that far from our preliminary figure for the 1920–92 period.

31 Figures for the other associations are too low for distributions over time to be meaningful. As already noted, the Quebec association admitted its first women members in the 1940s, which accounts for the different time periods covered in parts A and B of table B.18.

32 Note that we have omitted exits for those entering from 1990 forward since there was little opportunity for exits to occur prior to 1992, the cut-off date for our project.

33 It is possible that they were influenced by the difficulty, already mentioned, of becoming association members in the early years.

34 Gwendolyn Wright also recognizes that women architects, in particular, have been 'anonymous designers'; '*adjuncts* to the profession: planners, programmers, critics, writers, journalists'; or '*reformers* dedicated to creating alternatives.' She does not mention registration status, though she does underline that the *reformers* were 'altogether outside the profession' (1977, 284; emphasis in the original); it is quite possible that all these types of work have been undertaken by unregistered professionals.

35 Tim Kehoe, Executive Director, RAIC, personal communication, 3 September 1998.

36 RAIC mission statement quoted by its president in a RAIC newsletter update, June/July 1993.

37 This term should be elaborated. As the subsequent presentation of women architect's post-association employment suggests, we were looking for some commonality between architectural education and such employment. Thus, if we remember that architecture is *interdisciplinary* and if we remember Crossman's definition, cited in chapter 1, as encompassing 'artistic traditions,' 'techniques of science,' and 'managerial theories of modern business' (1987, 4), then we can see architectural qualifications as embracing artistic and technical expertise together with the relevant business experience. In this way, the commonality sought could be artistic or technical, as related to some form of construction, or, at the limit, business precepts applied to the housing/construction field.

38 Many non-registered architects pay registered architects to stamp their drawings. See chapter 4 for examples of women who worked as architects for extended periods without registering with a provincial association.

39 Note that we are dealing with *Quebec* women, and as a result the estimates for women differ slightly from those already cited for the sample of women as a whole, as indicated in table 2.6.

40 Whether the limited variability and innovation in men's post-association employment, as compared with women's, arises from the fact that a smaller group of men was interviewed is difficult to judge – but the men interviewed do appear to have channelled their energies into a limited range of employment.

3: Images in the Mirror

Versions of this chapter appeared as Adams 1994a and 1994c.

1 These details of Ebba Nilsson's life are drawn from *Histoire de Waterville ...* (1976, 50). I am grateful to Linda Ouellet of the Corporation Municipale de la Ville de Waterville for additional information on Ebba Nilsson.

2 Quebec's first woman architect was Pauline Roy Rouillard, recorded in the registrar's ledger at the OAQ; see Tremblay 1993a and 1993b.

3 The major published sources on Canadian women are van Ginkel 1991, 5–11, and an abridged version of the same article (November 1993, 15–17); see also Contreras, Ferrara, and Karpinski 1993. The histories of women architects in both the United States and Britain have inspired book-length studies. See, for example, Berkeley 1989, Cole 1973, Torre 1977, and Wright 1977. On British women, see Walker 1984. On the contributions of women to domestic architecture from outside the profession, see Hayden 1981.

4 The RAIC was founded in 1907. The journal was launched in January 1924 as the major publication of the RAIC. Its title changed to *Architecture Canada* in July 1966. The final issue was published in July 1973.

5 In general, material culture studies employ non-textual and non-verbal sources, particularly artefacts and objects, to discern historical, cultural, and social change. Unrelated to material culture, specific methodological models for exploring images of women in printed sources include Favro 1989 and Vipond 1977. See also des Rivières 1992.

6 On the impact of women in Canadian health professions, see Fahmy-Eid 1997, Mitchinson 1991, and Strong-Boag 1981. On women's attraction to preventive medicine, see Morantz-Sanchez 1985, 63.

7 The competitive nature of the field in Canada is noted in 'Opportunities for Young Architects ...' This was frequently cited as a reason to refuse admission to women, see Collins n.d., 12; a copy of this pamphlet is in the Peter Collins Collection, Canadian Architecture Collection, McGill University.

8 The reaction of Victorian feminists to these theories is voiced in 'Women Never Invent Anything' (1876).

9 For examples of this, see '"We Knew What We Wanted"' (1949); and Jukes 1946.

10 On Queen Anne architecture, see Girouard 1977; Maitland 1990; and Scully 1971. On the relationship of women's power to Queen Anne architecture in England, see Adams 1996b.

11 'Women as Architects' (1911).

12 See note 13. One woman expressed her frustration over the insensitivity of architects to her needs in Eden 1936, 17. Insightful observations on the association of women with houses is found in Hornstein-Rabinovitch 1990.

13 Rhoda and Agnes Garrett were the first professional women decorators in England; they were cousin and sister to two of the most visible feminists in the women's movement: political reformer Millicent Garrett Fawcett, and Elizabeth Garrett Anderson, the first woman physician in England. Their ideas were published in *Suggestions for House Decoration* (1876). On the feminization of interior decoration in England, see Neiswander 1988.

14 Beecher's house plan is the focus of many feminist analyses of U.S. domestic architecture. One of the earliest was Hayden 1981, 55–63.

15 Interior Designers of Ontario was established in 1933; in Quebec, the Société des designers d'interieur du Québec was founded two years later. See *Directory of Associations in Canada (1993–1994)*.

16 According to this literature, courses were offered at both McGill and the University of Toronto. The five-year McGill course was taught by Ramsay Traquair at $147/year. This reference is baffling, however, as the School of Architecture at McGill

did not accept a woman student until 1939. Blanche Lemco van Ginkel has suggested that women were accepted at McGill because of the dearth of students in the
1930s: 1991, 8, and personal letter from van Ginkel, 9 July 1993.

17 Dallaire's letter is reprinted in Collins n.d., 13. On the admission of women to
McGill, see Adams 1996a.

18 Similar concerns were expressed in Robson 1929, 1–3.

19 Osborne's comments appear in *RAIC Journal* 18/2 (February 1941): 20; on the
University of Manitoba, see 'Architectural Education ...' (1954) and *Architecture
Canada* 44/2 (February 1967): 63.

20 The series was broadcast on the Canadian Radio Commission Toronto (CRTC). See
Parry 1935. Cook's broadcast is mentioned in Simmins 1989, 112. The first article
written by a woman non-architect was by Jeannette Kilham, January 1928.

21 Cook 1935, 205. Cook later designed a number of kitchens to appear in Formica
trade literature. Cook's expertise in kitchen design was echoed a few decades later
when designer Sigrun Bulow-Hube was commissioned by the Canada Mortgage
and Housing Corporation to survey forty kitchens. See Hodges 1996.

22 See 'Award in RAIC Student Competitions,' *RAIC Journal* 11/3 (March 1934): 39.
A photo of work by a female student, Ethelyn Wallace, was published in March
1930. Also, the OAA prize had been awarded to a woman student, Beatrice Cent-
ncr, in June 1930.

23 Phyllis Cook Carlisle was included in the exhibition 'For the Record: Ontario
Women Graduates in Architecture 1920–1960,' which celebrated the 100th anniversary of the enrolment of women at the University of Toronto. The biographical
data cited here are drawn from the exhibition material.

24 Bauer's contributions are outlined in Friedan and Nash, Jr. 1969, 3–5.

25 See 'St. Joseph's High School, Toronto, Ont.,' *RAIC Journal* 27/11 (November
1950): 383.

26 See *RAIC Journal* 12/1 (January 1935): 13. Elliot advertised her services in the
popular press. See *Canadian Homes and Gardens* 6/7 (July 1929): 105.

27 See James 1947; a brief biographical sketch of James is offered in the same issue
(p. 285). For examples of James's design work, see 'North York Public Library,'
RAIC Journal 36/12 (December 1959): 412–17; and 'The Imperial Oil Building,'
RAIC Journal 34/7 (July 1957): 243–55. Her work also appeared in *Canadian
Homes and Gardens* 25/5 (May 1948): 32–3, 64; and *Saturday Night* 51 (29 Febru-
ary 1936): 9.

28 This 'pleasure' women supposedly derive from the design of interiors is also evident in the women's popular press. See, for example, the ad for paint, which states
'Decorating Is a New Thrill,' *Canadian Homes and Gardens* 27/5 (May 1950):
53.

29 For illustrations of buildings designed by Canadian women architects included in

secondary sources, see Contreras, Ferrara, and Karpinski 1993, Dominey 1992, and van Ginkel 1991.

30 Mary Clark's preliminary study of female students shows that the number of women graduates increased from 2.9 per cent during the 1960s, to 12.2 per cent and 25.1 per cent during the 1970s and 1980s, respectively (June 1988).

31 I am grateful to Linda Cohen for this insight.

32 A woman appeared in a similar advertisement for a water cooler in *RAIC Journal* 46/3 (March 1969): 65.

33 Advertisements for door hardware featured commercial settings as well. See the ad for shopping centre doors in *RAIC Journal* 44/1 (January 1967): 6–7; or for the corporate boardroom in ibid. 45/2 (February 1968): 26–7.

34 See the advertisement for Acousti-shell ceilings, for example, in *RAIC Journal* 41/7 (July 1964): 82–3; or the ad featuring twins for Pli-tone paint in ibid. 42/4 (April 1965): 34; or the woman on a stair surrounded by a lead barrier in ibid. 44/12 (December 1967): 13. Carpet ads are particularly common: see the image showing a woman descending a stair covered in wool carpet in ibid. 45/3 (March 1968): 68; the ad for Ozite carpets in ibid. 45/5 (May 1968): 29; and the ad for Armstrong carpets in ibid. 45/5 (May 1968): 24.

35 Another ad for smoke detectors featuring a nurse appeared in *RAIC Journal* 45/6 (June 1968): 34.

36 Other typical ads showing nurses include Johns-Manville acoustical ceilings in *RAIC Journal* 45/4 (April 1968): 54; Torginol flooring, ibid. 46/5 (May 1969): 32; and Corbin locks, ibid. 46/6 (June 1969): 13.

37 The first instance of a woman shown in collaboration with men appeared in the advertisement for Canadian Gypsum Company Ltd, shown in figure 3.2.

38 The difficulties faced by women on construction sites is a constant theme in the literature. See Kingsley and Glynn 1992, 15–16; Dixon 1989, 7; and 'Women in Corporate Firms,' *Architecture* 80/10 (October 1991): 82–3. See also chapter 5 of this book.

39 Photograph of Douglas Johnson, president of the OAA, and his wife, both wearing hardhats, in front of Toronto City Hall, *RAIC Journal* 42/4 (April 1965): 15.

40 Joynes 1959. The article first appeared in *Habitat* 11/4 (July-August 1959): 2–6, accompanied by eight illustrations of projects by Canadian women architects. Joynes was assistant to the National Director of the Community Planning Association of Canada; she was not an architect.

41 'To Women Architects,' *RAIC Journal* 41/11 (November 1964): 141.

42 'International Conference for Women,' *Architecture Canada* 47/546 (26 October 1970): 2.

43 On Wallbridge and Imrie Architects, see Contreras, Ferrara, and Karpinski 1993,

22–3, and Dominey 1992. Records of the firm are held by both the Provincial Museum and Archives of Alberta, Edmonton, and the City of Edmonton, Parks and Recreation. Mary Imrie was included in the exhibition 'For the Record.' Two of Wallbridge and Imrie's projects were illustrated in Joynes's article in *Habitat*, see note 40.

44 See 'House of Mr. J.A. Russell, Edmonton, Alberta,' *RAIC Journal* 30/2 (February 1953): 42–3; and 'Architects' Own Houses,' ibid. 36/2 (February 1959): 41. A large row-housing project was published in *The Canadian Architect* 2/2 (February 1957): 31–2.

45 Letter from Mary Imrie to Eric Arthur, dated 3 June 1954, Provincial Archives of Alberta, cited in Dominey 1992, 14.

46 See 'Planning in Europe,' *RAIC Journal* 25/10 (October 1948): 388–90; 'South American Architects,' 29/2 (February 1952): 29–31; 'Les Girls en Voyage,' ibid. 35/2 (February 1958): 44–6; 'Hong Kong to Chandigarh,' ibid. 35/5 (May 1958): 160–3; 'Khyber Pass to Canada,' ibid. 35/7 (July 1958): 278–9. Wallbridge's student entry to the RAIC competition was published in ibid. 16/4 (April 1939): 86, even though she was not the official winner; notice of Wallbridge's acceptance to the Alberta Association of Architects was remarked on in 'Provincial Page,' *RAIC Journal* 18/3 (March 1941): 52.

47 See 'Alberta' section of 'News from the Institute,' *RAIC Journal* 26/12 (December 1949): 448.

48 Contreras, Ferrara, and Karpinski note that 'much speculation was given to their free lifestyle' (1993, 23). Six Acres was illustrated in Joynes's article in *Habitat* (see note 40) and in *RAIC Journal* 36/2 (February 1959): 41; the notice of the firm's move was given in *RAIC Journal* 35/5 (May 1958): 196.

49 See the publication of McGill student work, which includes work by Blanche Lemco, and Catherine Chard, McGill's first woman student, *RAIC Journal* 19/2 (February 1942): 26.

50 See, for example, her article 'The Centre City Pedestrian,' *Architecture Canada* 45/8 (August 1968): 36–9; notices about her in *RAIC Journal* 33/12 (December 1956): 483; ibid. 38/1 (January 1961): 57; *Architecture Canada* 43/12 (December 1966): 67; ibid. 50/588 (June 1973): 4; ibid. 50/589 (July 1973): 4; ibid. 48/558 (10 May 1971): 17; ibid. 48/562 (12 July 1971): 4–5; photos of van Ginkel appeared in *RAIC Journal* 41/11 (November 1964): 35; ibid. 40/3 (March 1963): 89; and ibid. 45/12 (December 1968): 7.

51 O'Connor was elected in 1976. Cluff became a fellow in 1982.

52 See *RAIC Journal* 42/3 (March 1965): 85; and *Architecture Canada* 43/8 (August 1966): 5.

53 See 'Odds & Ends,' *The Canadian Architect* 5/3 (March 1960): 6.

54 Curriculum vitae of Pamela J. Cluff, dated January 1993; several photos of Cluff

appeared in the journal. See *Architecture Canada* 46/7–8 (July–August 1969): 10; ibid. 47/533 (16 March 1970): 2.

55 See 'Illustrations, Architects' Offices,' *RAIC Journal* 25/10 (October 1948): 370, 373, 377, 381–2.

56 The 1941 figure for men included those on active service. It should also be noted that the census category included 'architect' and 'building architect,' both of which presumably would be recognized by the profession. However, the category also included 'naval architect' (1941), and 'landscape architect' and 'landscape designer' (1951), all of which would be excluded by the profession's definition, as indicated in chapter 2, note 6.

57 The first woman assistant editor was Leah Gingras, BID. See *RAIC Journal* 39/12 (December 1962); Anita Aarons's first article for the journal appeared in January 1965): 55–6.

4: Building the Foundations

1 An overview of the careers of several of these women is offered in van Ginkel 1991.

2 One has to wonder whether a new look at the careers of U.S. and British women architects, with less emphasis on printed sources, might lead to similar conclusions.

3 'Expo 67,' *Architectural Record*, July 1967.

4 On Vecsei, see 'Architect's business is to sell dreams,' *The Gazette*, 16 February 1987, D1.

5 *Montreal Star*, 1965, on Vecsei.

6 'International Architects Named Honorary Fellows,' *American Institute of Architects Journal*, May 1990, 43.

7 Many of the best-known women architects in the United States in the post-war period were also immigrants from outside North America: Denise Scott Brown (born Zambia, educated South Africa and Europe), Susana Torre (born and educated Argentina), Anne Griswold Tyng (born China). The high percentage of foreign-born women architects in the United States is noted in Greer 1982, p. 47.

8 This is also true of other Canadian provinces. In British Columbia, for example, 77 per cent of women architects were immigrants in the pre-1970 period, as indicated in chapter 2.

9 Personal correspondence from Anne-Marie Balazs Pollowy, 23 August 1994. Tiiu Tammist O'Brien, a Lithuanian immigrant, also worked at ARCOP on Place Bonaventure.

10 On La Cité, see 'Hotel topped off,' *Montreal Star*, 3 January 1976, A10; 'La Cité,' *Architectural Record*, January 1978, 111–16.

11 DBC has undergone several changes of name; it was known as David Barott

Boulva (1961–4), David and Boulva (1964–73), and David Boulva Cleve (1973–93). It ceased to exist in 1993.

12 O'Brien was registered with the OAQ from 1962 to 1989.

13 Personal interview with Pauline Barrable, 29 July 1994.

14 Carol Moore Ede, 'Place Bonaventure,' *Canadian Architecture, 1960–70.*

15 '1960 Pilkington Travelling Scholarship and Awards,' *RAIC Journal*, August 1960, 338.

16 Personal correspondence from Blanche Lemco van Ginkel, dated 9 July 1993.

17 Telephone conversation with Vecsei, 14 September 1998.

18 See Brown 1989, 237–46.

19 Chenevert's career is well documented by Katia Tremblay (1993b, Ch. II).

20 We are grateful to Elspeth Cowell for providing us with information on Ilsa Williams. Cowell wrote her honours essay at Carleton University on W.F. Williams. Personal correspondence, 1 November 1993.

21 Personal letter from van Ginkel, 9 June 1995.

22 Personal letter from Walford, 3 January 1998.

23 The appeal to women architects of working directly with people is related to what some scholars have suggested is a feminine design sensibility, an assumption that women actually design differently from men. Other aspects of women's supposedly innate qualities, as manifested in design, include sensitivity to context, the ability to work in teams, more concern about social issues, and, perhaps the most damaging, a penchant for details. The latter is related, of course, to women's record in interior design. Such thinking, we believe, is both dangerous and unsubstantiated, and has worked against women's acceptance in the field (e.g., Kingsley 1988; Loyd 1975).

24 Like DBC, the office saw a number of name changes during this period; founded in 1912 as Barott & Blackader, it was subsequently called Barott, Marshall & Montgomery (1944–6); Barott, Marshall, Montgomery & Merrett (1946–57); Barott, Marshall & Merrett (1957–8); Barott, Marshall, Merrett & Barott (1958–61); Barott, Marshall & Merrett (1961–2); and Marshall & Merrett (1962–5). The firm is currently known as Nicolaidis Fukushima Orton Emmian. Since it is typically referred to as BMMB among Montreal architects, we use that name here.

25 For a description of the building, see 'Odds & Ends,' *The Canadian Architect* 10/8 (August 1965): 5–6.

26 Walford was interested in medicine before she even studied architecture; the results of her high-school career placement tests pointed to medicine or architecture. She chose architecture after having been disappointed at the attitude of medical schools to women in the profession: Personal letter from Dorice Walford, 19 November 1994.

27 Personal correspondence from Dorice Walford, 17 July 1995.

28 Telephone conversation with Art Nichol, 13 October 1995.

29 Canadian Centre for Architecture, 'Biographical Notes, Blanche Lemco van Ginkel.'

30 Personal letter from Walford, 3 January 1998.

31 Much of our information on Mactavish is from her son, Stuart Mactavish; a photograph of her appeared in *Architecture–Bâtiment–Construction*, February 1955, 43.

32 See Shaw 1956.

33 Personal letter from Walford, 19 November 1994.

34 For the full details of McGill's acceptance of women, see Adams 1996a. Biographical information on Chard Wisnicki may be found in *Constructing Careers ...* (1996, 43–9).

35 Personal letter from Chard Wisnicki, 25 October 1994.

36 Personal letter from Sherry McKay, 25 September 1995.

37 Personal letter from van Ginkel, 24 September 1995.

38 Personal letter from McKay, 25 September 1995.

39 A student project for a tourist information building was published in *RAIC Journal*, April 1939, 88.

40 In 1942, at the request of the federal government, Anglo-Canadian Pulp and Paper formed a shipbuilding company to take the pressure off the shipyards. See *Canada's War at Sea* (1944), I, 118.

41 These biographical details are taken from Mme Rouillard's curriculum vitae, dated 6 April 1994. For extensive information on her career, see Tremblay 1993b.

42 Letter from Helen Duchesne to Pauline Roy, 5 October 1942.

43 *RAIC Journal* 19/12 (December 1942): 239.

44 For an interesting account of her graduation see, 'First woman architect receives big ovation,' *Globe and Mail*, 5 June 1920, 8.

45 This biographical information on Hill is taken from Contreras, Ferrara, and Karpinski 1993, 18–23; while this article provides substantial information on Hill's career, her name is incorrect.

46 Many Ontario women architects were featured in the exhibition, 'For the Record,' University of Toronto, 1986.

47 Geoffrey Simmins (1989, 107) has implied that Kertland and Harris may have designed the house, even though Biriukova's name is on the drawings.

48 'A Canadian Artist's Modern Home,' *Canadian Homes and Gardens* 8/4 (April 1931): 40.

49 Personal correspondence from Robert Hill, 11 June 1993.

50 A photo of Humphreys (at that time her name was Humphrys) was published in *RAIC Journal* 24/4 (April 1947): 136.

51 Most of these biographical data are drawn from Humphreys's curriculum vitae, dated October 1993.
52 'Canadian Architects: Perks + Penny,' office portfolio, received April 1994.
53 Letter from Marilyn Robertson Lemieux to Margaret Gillett, n.d.
54 Kay Rex, remodels old houses, *Globe and Mail*, 25 October 1962.
55 'For the Record,' exhibition, 1986.
56 Information provided by the firm and Contreras (1994, 12).
57 Personal letter from Gail E. Lamb, dated 18 January 1994.
58 Lorenz 1990, 100–1; see Karpinski 1994, 13.
59 Quoted from material originally prepared for the exhibition 'For the Record,' faxed to us in August 1995.

5: Unregistered Professionals

1 Remember that a significant proportion of unregistered professionals will stem from the group of 'never registered' professionals – a group that unfortunately could not be included in the present research project.
2 As indicated in greater detail in Appendix A, given the small sample size and the extreme difficulty in contacting respondents, the fit between the sample and the original population is not perfect. In addition, as has been mentioned, the very small number of women de-registering from the Atlantic provinces' associations over the total research period (four) could not be reflected within the sample (table 2.4, column 2). Nevertheless, the general 'fit' between the sample and the original population ensures that women of various age groups and regional origins are represented within the discussion.
3 Though the interview material is revealing about subtle influences: 'She's [her mother] had to work hard her whole life, but [she's] a wonderful artist ... crocheting and creating quilts and ... gardens. Just like she was an extremely creative person and a big influence on me because she read me lots of stories of the artists and what-not ... she didn't think she did it because she thought she'd make me into something but just because she loved these things' (F:24).
4 This respondent volunteered that three of her four brothers were also builders (F:8).
5 A very short one, we might add; she graduated in 1989.
6 The literature generally suggests that women in the male-dominated professions are more likely than their male colleagues to be single and childless (Armstrong and Armstrong 1992, 130; Rinfret 1997, 10). Symons (1984, 341) cites very high proportions (between 40 per cent and 50 per cent) of her samples of Canadian and French managers who were single, separated, or divorced, and childless.
7 Not surprisingly, most of the women with this family size are from earlier cohorts, that is, graduating pre-1975. The average family size for all respondents is just

under two; the fertility rate has been 1.7 to 1.8 births per woman since the late 1970s (Lero and Johnson 1994, 11).

8 As Hagan and Kay point out, two-thirds of the men, but only one-third of the women in their Ontario sample were parents (1995, 104). Marshall emphasizes that women in male-dominated professions are less likely than others to be part of a family or to have children (1989, 14).

9 One-third graduated from McGill, one-third from Montreal, and the final third from Laval and other institutions outside Quebec. McGill graduates, in particular, do not necessarily stay in Quebec and can be found elsewhere in Canada.

10 We are not counting the so-called B.Sc. Arch. from McGill as a first degree (after three years), followed by the B. Arch. after the fourth year of study. It seems that this arrangement, of convenience rather than substance, was introduced to satisfy the Quebec government's requirement that a degree be granted after three years: N. Schoenhauer, personal communication.

11 It should be noted that the Groat and Ahrentzen sample is strongly slanted towards tenured women (55 per cent) for reasons specific to their study. They provide no breakdown by year of first degree or age, and it is possible that their sample of faculty women is older than our sample of de-registered professionals, and thus not comparable. But given that our respondents cover the past fifty years of architectural experience, though admittedly a high proportion graduated in the 1970s and 1980s, and that academic women in architecture are a recent addition to the academy, the two samples are unlikely to differ significantly in terms of age.

12 Higher degrees are, in fact, very frequent; over half of all respondents and three-quarters of the cohorts from the 1960s and 1970s (who have had enough time to undertake further study) hold higher degrees. This experience is more common among anglophone (nearly two-thirds) than francophone respondents (just over one-third); on the other hand, all francophones, if they do continue academic work, go onto a third degree, which is rare among anglophones.

13 Unfortunately, we do not have parallel data on *registered* architects for purposes of comparison. It should be noted that such responsibilities went well beyond children and partners/spouses. The women respondents often talked of parents and in-laws as part of their responsibilities or, as respondent F:19 explains: 'In 1973, my husband decided he was going to buy a dairy farm ... and I was then responsible for fifty-four cows ... a lot of work goes into a dairy farm, my husband was off working all of the time and so it was a major responsibility for me ... I think it's fair to say that it was a very stressful twenty or thirty years.'

14 It is difficult to know how accurate are our data on unemployment. Given the way that our respondents were contacted (we indicated that we wished to interview architects who had de-registered from their provincial associations), it is possible that those with long periods of unemployment or those who were unemployed at

the time of the interviews hesitated to agree to be interviewed. On the other hand, the eight women who reported periods of unemployment, ranging from two to eight years, did not seem embarrassed in speaking to us. It was also clear that the respondents expected far more questions about the associations and less investigation of the details of their careers than, in fact, characterized the interviews.

15 In 1994, 26 per cent of all women with jobs were employed part-time, in comparison with just 9 per cent of employed men (Statistics Canada 1995, 65).

16 As respondent M:3 admits: 'Plus tard, j'ai travaillé à mon compte. Ça veut dire que j'étais en chômage [rires].' ('Later, I was self-employed, which means that I was unemployed [laughs]').

17 The dates were obtained from the records of provincial associations. Respondent M:3: 'Q: Parce que je remarque que vous étiez membre de '84 à '88, à peu près? R: Je ne me rappelle pas exactement' (Q: 'I notice that you were a member from approximately 1984 to 1988? R: 'I don't remember'). Respondent F:14: 'Q: Do you happen to remember what year you entered into l'Ordre des Architectes du Québec?' A: 'No.'

18 Respondent F:9: 'Then, what's important, too, in the architectural career is that I passed my OAQ exam'; Respondent F:18: 'moi, j'ai fait, et c'est écrit: "Reçue aux examens de l'Ordre en '92."' ('what I did, and I have it in writing: "Passed the examination of the Order in 1992"').

19 We have already mentioned women's propensity for work in the public sector in chapter 4.

20 Citing an hourly wage of $16 in 1991.

21 This term, of course, comes from the service sector and refers to the managerial practice (e.g., in supermarkets) of hiring just enough personnel to cover the needs of the enterprise at a particular time.

22 Salaman also mentions the disappointment that arises from the lack of opportunities to participate in design (quoted in Blau 1984, 59).

23 A couple of respondents did mention the approach to work. Respondent F:11, for example, explained that she preferred a more theoretical and reflective approach to architecture – which she eventually found in art history; respondent F:21 was attracted by the more categorical nature of engineering, and she went on to take degrees in civil engineering. (We will return to this theme in the discussion of the men's interviews.) But most of the comments signified an acceptance of the nature of architecture as conveyed in architectural training – but a rejection of how this translated into workplace practice.

24 The consequences of a second rather than a first child are also mentioned in the literature, for example by Marchis-Mouren, Giasson, and Martel (1990, 96).

25 On the other hand, they do provide evidence of spouses/partners who *add* to their working responsibilities. For example, as already cited, respondent F:19 had to

look after a dairy farm; respondent F:28 states that her husband's real estate invest-
ments needed committed supervision; respondent F:1 was needed in her husband's
business. However, none of this could be considered 'domestic work' in the sense
of caring and providing for a spouse or partner.

26 This is undoubtedly a commentary on the gradual evolution of household tasks;
responsibilities for the spouse are eroded first, whereas child-care responsibilities
remain a major task for professional women.

27 As we will see, none of the male respondents comment on family or child-care
responsibilities; our women respondents obviously live in an environment where
these traditional responsibilities are still accorded to them.

28 One of the men interviewed was disabled, but this condition clearly predated his
work in architecture and was not linked to working conditions in the profession.

29 As we saw (note 23), this was a rare reaction on the part of the women.

30 Though it should be noted that all the women who chose alternative employment,
at least in part for financial reasons, were from Quebec; perhaps the Quebec
women and men are reflecting an even more dire economic situation within their
province. This is the only way in which Quebec women stand out from their colleagues from other provinces in the themes they chose to emphasize.

31 This rather ugly expression stems from the world of women managers, some of
whom, it is argued, choose to devote considerable energy to their families and thus,
cannot be considered for the all-encompassing 'normal track' of managerial
careers.

32 Because we had not anticipated the result that the de-registered professionals were
not, in fact, leaving architecture at the beginning of the series of interviews, a direct
question on this topic was not part of all the interviews. Thus, these comments are
either spontaneous, or result from later interviews in the series.

33 About 10 per cent of all respondents.

6: The Quebec Question

1 As Linteau, et al. (1991, 307) point out, this term has two meanings – a strict meaning referring to provincial government reforms undertaken between 1960 and 1966,
and a wider meaning referring to the 1960s and 1970s. We intend the latter meaning, though, as will be seen, there are some modifications in the mid-1970s.

2 This expression is used to indicate that the proportion of women architects, both
registered and unregistered, is a little higher than one might expect on the basis of
the population of Quebec (25 per cent in 1991: *Canada Year Book 1997*, Table 3.2).

3 Of course, the rates of exit are preliminary for both provinces, but provide some
indication of differing patterns for Quebec and Ontario.

4 It should be noted that their Ontario women colleagues *leave* their association more

rapidly because of a higher rate of mobility to other associations and a higher rate of retirement and death (they are, of course, older than the Quebec women) (cf. table 2.4). In conjunction with the very high rate of entry of Quebec women to their provincial association, this would help to explain the fact that the Quebec women dominate female architectural practice in Canada.

5 Couture (1988) espouses a version of this hypothesis that emphasizes technological rather than social change, but does not contradict the argument in this chapter.

6 Personal communication, 24 January 1996.

7 This is not intended to negate the argument about the contribution of immigrant women that has been put forward in chapters 2 and 4. That they took the lead is undeniable; but that they were chosen to lead in the kind of context outlined also holds true.

8 We use this term rather than the more common term 'rattrapage,' or 'catching up,' for the very good reason that, as we have noted, the pattern includes more than catching up; in fact, what is remarkable about the Quebec pattern for women architects is that the women overtake their Canadian colleagues in the other provinces rather than merely hurrying after them. It is perhaps for this reason that contemporary historians are more hesitant to use the term; however, it is still used, for example in McRoberts 1988, 129–30.

9 Dumont is a little generous in citing this early date for the rest of Canada. In fact, the first woman in the British Empire to graduate from a university did so at Mount Allison University in New Brunswick in 1875, entering the university in 1873. However, women were admitted as early as 1869 to Queen's University, though the first woman did not graduate from Queen's until 1885 (Legendre 1981, 64, 66). As for Quebec women, 1907 signals the institution of a classical college for girls, the only means of access to university education at the time; their entry to university would necessarily come slightly later (Susan Mann, personal communication).

10 Though the term is being questioned at the moment; for example, Bourque (1995, 47) talks of 'la vieille thèse du retard' ('the ancient thesis of lateness').

11 This statement is by no means intended to deny the significant effort on the part of some Quebec women, particularly Thérèse Casgrain, to obtain suffrage for Quebec women, nor to deny the significance of women's suffrage for later generations of Quebec women who have clearly valued and celebrated their right to vote. It merely suggests that, for the period leading up to 1940, the issue of women's suffrage did not play a similar role within Quebec as it had done in the early twentieth century in the rest of Canada.

12 In all cases, surpassed by no other province (physicians) or by only one or two small provinces, where the absolute number of women is very low and where the 'random rounding' to a multiple of 5, which is employed by the Canadian census, might affect percentages. All comparisons are based on census material

since parallel data for registered professionals are not available for all these professions; however, a team of researchers is presently working on the engineering profession (Tancred et al. 1994) and undoubtedly similar data on the other professions
will eventually become available.

13 Hagan and Kay also note this contrast between Quebec and Ontario lawyers (1995,
11). However, they express the comparison rather differently, by indicating that the
legal profession, up to 1971, was much more male-dominated in Quebec than in
English Canada. As of 1981, and after, the profession in Ontario became more
male-dominated than in Quebec. We presume that they are basing their statements
on census data (our own calculations would so indicate), though no references are
given.

14 For a full treatment see Linteau et al. 1991, ch. 30–54.

15 In fact, nearly 80 per cent of all Quebec women who exited their provincial association de-registered in the period 1975–89.

16 Remember that post-1969 entrants to both the Ontario and Quebec provincial associations were much more likely to de-register earlier in their careers than their pioneering counterparts (see chapter 2).

17 Sadly, this is the only page, in a book-length work on the professions, where the
subject of women is raised!

18 For an empirical example of this process of ensuring 'a similarity of background'
in professional recruits, and how this affects women candidates, please see
Schirmer and Tancred 1996.

19 Ringon (n.d., 19), for France, notes that architectural practice in that country is
widening to include 'neighbouring domains,' and even areas 'outside' architecture,
such as design, 'conception,' and graphics.

20 This phrase is based on Ursula Franklin's title for her CRIAW publication: *Will
Women Change Technology or Will Technology Change Women?* (1985).

Appendix A: Methodology

1 The Territories were excluded from our coverage because of the very low number
of architects within their jurisdiction, of whom a negligible proportion have been
women. In addition, there is no association structure within the Territories.

2 Association terminology differs but in addition to being a full member, it is also
possible, for example, to be an Associate member, Retired member or Honourary
member. We also asked for the relevant definitions of such categories of affiliation.

Bibliography

ACFAS [Association canadienne-française pour l'avancement des sciences]. 1993. *Les Bâtisseuses de la Cité*. Montreal: Université de Montréal, Congrès de l'Acfas.

Acker, Joan. 1992. 'Gendering Organizational Theory.' In *Gendering Organizational Analysis*, ed. Albert Mills and Peta Tancred, 248–60. Newbury Park, CA: Sage.

ACSA [Association of Collegiate Schools of Architecture] Task Force on the Status of Women. 1990. *The Status of Faculty Women in Architecture Schools*. Washington, DC: ACSA.

Adam, Peter. 1987. *Eileen Gray: Architect/Designer*. London: Thames and Hudson.

Adams, Annmarie. 1994a. 'Building Barriers: Images of Women in the *RAIC Journal*, 1924–73.' *Resources for Feminist Research* 23/3 (Fall): 11–23.

– 1994b. 'Doctors as Architects: The Systematic View of the House, 1870–1900.' Paper delivered at American Historical Association, San Francisco, 8 January.

– 1994c. 'Les Representations des femmes dans la revue de l'Institut Royal Architectural du Canada, 1924–73.' *Recherches féministes* 7/2: 7–36.

– 1994d. 'Rooms of Their Own: The Nurses' Residences at Montréal's Royal Victoria Hospital.' *Material History Review* 40 (Fall): 29–41.

– 1995. 'The Eichler Home: Intention and Experience in Postwar Suburbia.' In *Gender, Class, and Shelter: Perspectives in Vernacular Architecture, V*, ed. Elizabeth Collins Cromley and Carter L. Hudgins, 164–78. Knoxville: University of Tennessee Press.

– 1996a. '"Archi-ettes" in Training: The Admission of Women to McGill's School of Architecture.' *Society for the Study of Architecture in Canada Bulletin* 21/3 (September): 70–3.

– 1996b. *Architecture in the Family Way: Doctors, Houses, and Women, 1870–1900*. Montreal and Kingston: McGill-Queen's University Press.

– 1996c. '"The House and All That Goes On in It": The Notebook of Frederica Shanks.' *Winterthur Portfolio* 31 (Summer/Autumn): 165–72.

Adams, Annmarie, and Peter Gossage. 1998. 'Chez Fadette: Girlhood, Family, and Private Space in Late-Nineteenth-Century Saint-Hyacinthe.' *Urban History Review* 26/2 (March): 56–68.

Adams, Annmarie, and Peta Tancred. 1996. 'McGill Export Helped Built B.C. Modernism.' *Gazette* (Montreal), 8 June, H5.

Adams, Tracey L. 1997. 'A Dentist and a Gentleman: The Significance of Gender to the Establishment of the Dental Profession.' PhD diss., University of Toronto.

'The Admission of Lady Associates.' 1898–9. *Journal of the Royal Institute of British Architects* 6/3 (10 December 1898): 77–8; and no. 9 (11 March 1899): 278–81.

Ahrentzen, Sherry, and Linda N. Groat. 1992. 'Rethinking Architectural Education: Patriarchal Conventions and Alternative Visions from the Perspective of Women Faculty.' *Journal of Architectural and Planning Research* 9 (Summer): 95–111.

Ainley, Marianne Gosztonyi. 1996. 'Les femmes dans les sciences au Canada: y a-t-il une division sexuelle du travail?' In *Femmes et Sciences: Au coeur des débats institutionnels et épistémologiques*, ed. L. Dumais and V. Boudreau, 3–18. Ottawa: ACFAS-Outaouais.

Allen, Polly Wynn. 1988. *Building Domestic Liberty: Charlotte Perkins Gilman's Architectural Feminism*. Amherst: University of Massachusetts Press.

Anderson, Dorothy May. 1980. *Women, Design and the Cambridge School*. West Lafayette, IN: PDA Publishers.

Andrew, Caroline, and Beth Moore Milroy, eds. 1988. *Life Spaces: Gender, Household, Employment*. Vancouver: UBC Press.

Anscombe, Isabelle. 1984. *A Woman's Touch: Women in Design from 1860 to the Present Day*. New York: Viking.

'Architect's Business Is to Sell Dreams.' 1987. *Gazette* (Montreal), 16 February, D1.

Architectural Design. 1975. 45/8.

'Architectural Education at the University of Manitoba 1913–1953.' 1954. *RAIC Journal* 31/3 (March): 63.

Architecture Canada. Royal Architectural Institute of Canada. July 1966–July 1973.

Architecture Minnesota. 1997. (July/August).

Armstrong, Pat, and Hugh Armstrong. 1992. 'Sex and the Professions in Canada.' *Journal of Canadian Studies* 27/1 (Spring): 118–33.

Arthur, Eric. 1986. *Toronto: No Mean City*. Toronto: University of Toronto Press.

Attfield, Judy, and Pat Kirkham, eds. 1989. *A View from the Interior: Feminism, Women and Design*. London: Women's Press.

Baker, Sarah. 1996. 'Professional Architectural Education: Women Articulate Masculinist Values.' Paper delivered at Canadian Women's Studies Association Conference, Brock University, St Catharines, May.

Banham, Reyner. 1976. *Megastructure: Urban Futures of the Recent Past*. London: Thames and Hudson.

Beecher, Catharine, and Harriet Beecher Stowe. 1869. *The American Woman's Home*. New York: Ford.

Berkeley, Ellen Perry, ed. 1989. *Architecture: A Place for Women*. Washington, DC: Smithsonian Institution.

Blau, Judith R. 1984. *Architects and Firms: A Sociological Perspective on Architectural Practice*. Cambridge, MA: MIT Press.

Bourque, Gilles. 1995. 'Du révisionnisme en histoire du Québec.' *Bulletin d'histoire politique* 4/2: 45–51.

Boutelle, Sarah Holmes. 1988. *Julia Morgan Architect*. New York: Abbeville.

Boyd, Monica. 1975. 'The Status of Immigrant Women in Canada.' *Canadian Review of Sociology and Anthropology* 12/4: 406–16.

Boys, Jos. 1984. 'Is There a Feminist Analysis of Architecture?' *The Built Environment* 10/1 (1 November): 25–34.

'A Brief History of the RAIC.' 1962. *RAIC Journal* 39/12 (December): 69–74.

Brown, Denise Scott. 1989. 'Sexism and the Star System in Architecture.' In *Architecture: A Place for Women*, ed. Ellen Perry Berkeley, 237–46. Washington, DC: Smithsonian Institution.

Buchner-Jeziorska, Anna, and Julia Evetts. 1997. 'Regulating Professionals: The Polish Example.' *International Sociology* 12/1: 61–72.

Buckley, Cheryl. 1986. 'Made in Patriarchy: Toward a Feminist Analysis of Women and Design.' *Design Issues* 3/2 (Fall): 3–24.

Burrage, Michael, Konrad Jarausch, and Hannes Siegrist. 1990. 'An Actor-Based Framework for the Study of the Professions.' In *Professions in Theory and History: Rethinking the Study of the Professions*, ed. Michael Burrage and Rolf Torstendahl, 203–25. London: Sage.

Bussel, Abby. 1995. 'Women in Architecture: Leveling the Playing Field.' *Progressive Architecture*, November, 45–9, 86.

Callen, Anthea. 1979. *Angel in the Studio: Women in the Arts and Crafts Movement, 1870–1914*. London: Astragal.

Canada. 1921–91. *Census of Canada*.

Canada Year Book 1997. 1996. Ottawa: Statistics Canada.

Canada's War at Sea. 1944. 2 vols. Montreal: A.M. Beatty.

Canadian Council of Professional Engineers. 1994–5. Data Bank.

Canadian Homes and Gardens. 1925–61.

Carrier, Sylvie. 1995. 'Family Status and Career Situation for Professional Women.' *Work, Employment and Society* 9/2: 343–58.

Carrière, Gabrielle. 1946. *Careers for Women in Canada: A Practical Guide*. Toronto: Dent.

Caven, Valerie. 1998. 'Building on the Middle Ground: Alternatives to Polarisation in

Women's Professional Employment.' Paper delivered at Gender, Work and Organisation Conference, Manchester, January.

Chard, Catherine. 1942. 'What Is an Architect?' *RAIC Journal* 19/2 (February): 30–3.

'La Cité.' 1978. *Architectural Record* (January): 111–16.

Clark, Mary. 1988. 'Registration of Women Architects in Canada: The Results of a Survey.' Toronto: University of Toronto. Mimeograph.

– June 1988. 'Women Graduates in Architecture from Canadian Universities: A Preliminary Overview.' Toronto: University of Toronto. Mimeograph.

Cole, Doris. 1973. *From Tipi to Skyscraper: A History of Women in Architecture.* Boston: i press.

– 1981. *Eleanor Raymond, Architect.* Philadelphia: Art Alliance Press.

Cole, Doris, and Karen Cord Taylor. 1990. *The Lady Architects: Lois Lilley Howe, Eleanor Manning and Mary Almy, 1893–1937.* New York: Midmarch Arts.

Le Collectif Clio. 1992. *L'Histoire des femmes au Québec depuis quatre siècles.* Montreal: Le Jour.

Collin, Johanne. 1992. 'Les femmes dans la profession pharmaceutique au Québec: rupture ou continuité?' *Recherches féministes* 5/2: 31–56.

Collins, Peter. n.d. *Notes on the Centenary of the Faculty of Engineering of McGill University: Its Origin and Growth.* N.p.: N.p.

Constructing Careers: Profiles of Five Early Women Architects in British Columbia. 1996. Vancouver: Women in Architecture Exhibits Committee, in Cooperation with the Architectural Institute of British Columbia.

Contreras, Monica. 1994. 'New Canadians.' *Ontario Association of Architects* (Spring): 12.

Contreras, Monica, Luigi Ferrara, and Daniel Karpinski. 1993. 'Breaking In: Four Early Female Architects.' *Canadian Architect* 38 (November): 18–23.

Cook, Phyllis Willson. 1935. 'The Modern Kitchen.' *RAIC Journal* 12/12 (December): 205.

Couture, Denise. 1988. 'Technologies médicales et statut des corps professionnels dans la division du travail socio-sanitaire.' *Sociologie et Sociétés* 20/2: 77–89.

Crompton, Rosemary. 1987. 'Gender, Status and Professionalism.' *Sociology* 21/3: 413–28.

Crossman, Kelly. 1987. *Architecture in Transition: From Art to Practice, 1885–1906.* Montreal and Kingston: McGill-Queen's University Press.

Cuff, Dana. 1991. *Architecture: The Story of Practice.* Cambridge, MA: MIT Press.

D'Augerot-Arend, Sylvie. 1991. 'Why So Late? Cultural and Institutional Factors in the Granting of Quebec and French Women's Political Rights.' *Journal of Canadian Studies* 26 (Spring): 138–65.

Davies, Celia. 1996. 'The Sociology of Professions and the Profession of Gender.'
    Sociology 30/4: 661–78.
– 1998. 'Gender and Race, Class and Age: The Decomposition of the Professional
    Ideal.' Paper delivered at International Sociological Association Congress, Montreal,
    July.
– Forthcoming. 'The Masculinity of Organisational Life.' In *Women and Public
    Policy: The Shifting Boundaries between the Public and Private*, ed. S. Baker and A.
    Van Doorne-Huiskes. London: Ashgate.
Dean, Andrea O. 1982. 'Women in Architecture: Individual Profiles and a Discussion
    of Issues.' *AIA Journal* (January): 42–51.
Dendy, William, and William Kilbourn. 1986. *Toronto Observed: Its Architecture,
    Patrons, and History.* Toronto: Oxford University Press.
Denis, Ann. 1981. 'Femmes: ethnie et occupation au Québec et en Ontario, 1931–
    1971.' *Canadian Ethnic Studies* 13/1: 75–90.
'Department of Interior Design 1966–67 University of Manitoba.' 1967. *Architecture
    Canada* 44/2 (February): 63.
Després, Carole, and Denise Piché. 1993. 'Partie A Section 3. Description de la recher-
    che ou de l'activité proposée.' Ottawa: Social Sciences and Humanities Research
    Council.
des Rivières, Marie-Josée. 1992. *Châtelaine et la Littérature (1960–1975).* Montreal:
    Éditions de l'Hexagone.
Dickinson, John A., and Brian Young. 1993. *A Short History of Quebec.* Toronto: Copp
    Clark Pitman.
Directory of Associations in Canada (1993–1994). Toronto: Canadian Almanack &
    Directory Pub. Co.
Dixon, John Morris. 1989. 'Women's Place in Architecture.' *Progressive Architecture*
    70 (October): 7.
– 1994. 'A White Gentleman's Profession?' *Progressive Architecture* 75 (November):
    55–61.
Dominey, Erna. 1992. 'Wallbridge and Imrie: The Architectural Practice of Two
    Edmonton Women, 1950–1979.' *Society for the Study of Architecture in Canada
    Bulletin* 17/1 (March): 12–18.
Drummond, Anne. 1978. 'Women in the McGill School of Architecture.' Unpublished
    paper.
Dumont, Micheline. 1992. 'The Origins of the Women's Movement in Québec.' In
    Challenging Times: The Women's Movement in Canada and the United States, ed.
    Constance Backhouse and David H. Flaherty, 72–89. Montreal and Kingston:
    McGill-Queen's University Press.
Eden, Louis. 1936. 'Architects Should Wear Skirts.' *Saturday Night* 52 (10 October):
    15.

Ehrenreich, Barbara, and Deirdre English. 1979. *For Her Own Good: 150 Years of the Experts' Advice to Women*. London: Pluto.

Erlemann, Christine. 1986. 'What Is Feminist Architecture?' In *Feminist Aesthetics*, ed. Gisela Ecker, 125–34. Boston: Beacon.

'Expo 67.' 1967. *Architectural Record* (July): 116–26.

Fahmy-Eid, Nadia. 1997. *Femmes, santé et professions*. Montreal: FIDES.

Faludi, E.G., and Catherine Chard. 1945. 'The Prefabricated House Industry.' *RAIC Journal* 22/3 (March): 56–62.

Favro, Diane. 1989. 'Ad-Architects.' In *Architecture: A Place for Women*, ed. Ellen Perry Berkeley, 187–200. Washington, DC: Smithsonian Institution.

– 1991. 'A Region for Women: Architects in Early California.' *Architecture California* 13/1 (February): 48–53.

– 1992. 'Sincere and Good: The Architectural Practice of Julia Morgan.' *The Journal of Architectural and Planning Research* 9/2 (Summer): 112–28.

Feldman, Roberta. 1989. *Research Plan for the Study of Attrition Rates of Women Architects*. Prepared for Women in Architecture Committee, American Institute of Architects. Mimeograph.

'For the Record: Ontario Women Graduates in Architecture 1920–1960.' 1986. Exhibition. University of Toronto, September-October.

Franck, Karen, and Sherry Ahrentzen, eds. 1989. *New Households, New Housing*. New York: Van Nostrand Reinhold.

Franklin, Ursula. 1985. *Will Women Change Technology or Will Technology Change Women?* Ottawa: Canadian Research Institute for the Advancement of Women.

Friedan, Bernard J., and William W. Nash, Jr, eds. 1969. *Shaping an Urban Future: Essays in Memory of Catherine Bauer Wurster*. Cambridge, MA: MIT Press.

Friedan, Betty. 1963. *The Feminine Mystique*. New York: Norton.

Garrett, Rhoda, and Agnes Garrett. 1876. *Suggestions for House Decoration*. London: Macmillan.

Giller, Doris. 1965. 'Architect stresses need for individuality in design.' *Montreal Star*, 19 August, 20.

Gillett, Margaret. 1981. *We Walked Very Warily: A History of Women at McGill*. Montreal: Eden.

Girouard, Mark. 1977. *Sweetness and Light: The Queen Anne Movement, 1860–1900*. Oxford: Clarendon Press.

Greer, Nora Richter. 1982. 'Women in Architecture: A Progress (?) Report and a Statistical Profile.' *AIA Journal* (January): 40–51.

Groat, Linda, and Sherry B. Ahrentzen. 1997. 'Voices for Change in Architectural Education: Seven Facets of Transformation from the Perspective of Faculty Women.' *Journal of Architectural Education* 50 (May): 271–85.

Hagan, John, and Fiona Kay. 1995. *Gender in Practice: A Study of Lawyers' Lives*. New York: Oxford University Press.

Haweis, Mrs H.R. 1881. *The Art of Decoration*. London: Chatto and Windus.

Hayden, Dolores. 1981. *The Grand Domestic Revolution: A History of Feminist Designs for American Homes, Neighborhoods and Cities*. Cambridge, MA: MIT Press.

– 1984. *Redesigning the American Dream: The Future of Housing, Work, and Family Life*. New York: Norton.

Histoire de Waterville/The History of Waterville. 1976. Waterville: The Townships Sun.

Hodges, Margaret. 1996. 'Sigrun Bulow-Hube: Scandinavian Modernism in Canada.' MA in Art History thesis, Concordia University.

Holmwood, John, and Janet Siltanen. 1994–5. 'Gender, the Professions, and Employment Citizenship.' *International Journal of Sociology* 24 (Winter): 43–66.

Hornstein-Rabinovitch, Shelly. 1990. 'The House That Jack Built.' *Canadian Woman Studies* 11/1 (Spring): 65–7.

'Hotel topped off.' 1976. *Montreal Star*, 3 January, A10.

Howe, Barbara J. 1992. 'Women and Architecture.' In *Reclaiming the Past: Landmarks of Women's History*, ed. Page Putnam Miller, 27–62. Bloomington: Indiana University Press.

'Interim Report on Study on Aims, Function and Structure of the Royal Architectural Institute of Canada.' 1965. Mimeograph.

Jacobs, Jerry. 1989. *Revolving Doors: Sex Segregation and Women's Careers*. Stanford, CA: Stanford University Press.

James, Freda G. 1947. 'How I Approach the Use of Colour.' *RAIC Journal* 24/8 (August): 280–1.

Joynes, Jennifer R. 1959. 'Women in the Architectural Profession.' *RAIC Journal* 36/9 (September): 320–1.

Jukes, Mary. 1946. 'Renovation Turned That into This.' *Canadian Homes and Gardens* 23/12 (December): 44–7, 60.

Kalman, Harold. 1994. *A History of Canadian Architecture*, 2 vols. Oxford: Oxford University Press.

Karpinski, Daniel. 1994. 'Helga Plumb.' *Ontario Association of Architects* (Spring): 13.

Kettle, John, and S.J. Cohen. 1958. 'The Architect's Office: Facts and Figures.' *Canadian Architect* (September): 53–60.

Kingsley, Karen. 1988. 'Gender Issues in Teaching Architectural History.' *Journal of Architectural Education* (Winter): 21–5.

– and Anne Glynn. 1992. 'Women in the Architectural Workplace.' *Journal of Architectural Education* 46/1 (September): 14–20.

Kinnear, Mary. 1995. *In Subordination: Professional Women, 1870–1970*. Montreal and Kingston: McGill-Queen's University Press.

Legendre, Anne Carmelle. 1981. 'The Baptist Contribution to Nineteenth Century Education for Women: An Examination of Moulton College and McMaster University.' MA thesis, McMaster University.

Lero, Donna S., and Karen L. Johnson. 1994. *Canadian Statistics on Work and Family*. Ottawa: Canadian Advisory Council on the Status of Women.

Linteau, Paul-André, René Durocher, Jean-Claude Robert, and François Ricard. 1991. *Quebec since 1930*. Toronto: James Lorimer.

Liscombe, Rhodri Windsor. 1985. 'Modes of Modernizing: The Acquisition of Modernist Design in Canada.' *Society for the Study of Architecture in Canada Bulletin* 10/3: 65.

– 1997. *The New Spirit: Modern Architecture in Vancouver, 1938–1963*. Vancouver: Douglas and McIntyre, in association with the Canadian Centre for Architecture.

L.M.H. 1875. *Year-book of Women's Work*.

Lorenz, Clare. 1990. *Women in Architecture: A Contemporary Perspective*. New York: Rizzoli.

Loyd, Bonnie. 1975. 'Woman's Place, Man's Place.' *Landscape* 20/1 (October): 10–13.

Lupton, Ellen. 1993. *Mechanical Brides: Women and Machines from Home to Office*. Princeton, NJ: Princeton Architectural Press.

Lupton, Ellen, and J. Abbot Miller. 1992. *The Bathroom, the Kitchen, and the Aesthetics of Waste: A Process of Elimination*. Cambridge, MA: MIT Visual Arts Center.

Maitland, Leslie. 1990. *The Queen Anne Revival Style in Canadian Architecture*. Ottawa: Minister of Supply and Services Canada.

Mangiacasale, Angela. 1985. 'Lily Inglis: The People's Architect.' *The Whig-Standard Magazine* (Kingston, ON), 23 March, 4–9.

Marchis-Mouren, Marie-Françoise, Francine Harel Giasson, and Louise Martel. 1990. 'Travail et maternité chez les jeunes femmes comptables agréées.' In *Actes de la Section d'Études féministes du Congrès de l'Acfas 1989*, 87–99. Montreal: Université du Québec à Montréal.

Marshall, Katherine. 1989. 'Women in Professional Occupations: Progress in the 1980s.' *Canadian Social Trends* (Spring): 13–15.

Massey, Alice Vincent. 1920. *Occupations for Trained Women in Canada*. London and Toronto: J.M. Dent.

Matrix. 1984. *Making Space: Women and the Man-made Environment*. London: Pluto.

McDougall, Anne. 1988. 'John Bland and the McGill School of Architecture.' *Canadian Architect* 15/3 (March): 33–7.

McMurry, Sally. 1989. 'Women in the American Vernacular Landscape.' *Material Culture* (Spring): 33–48.

McRoberts, Kenneth. 1988. *Social Change and Political Crisis*. Toronto: McClelland & Stewart.

Millar, Lillian D. 1945. 'Careers: Dentistry Profession in Which Women Could Excel.' *Saturday Night* 60 (11 August): 31.

Mitchell, Juliet. 1986. 'Reflections on Twenty Years of Feminism.' In *What Is Feminism?* ed. Juliet Mitchell and Ann Oakley, 34–48. New York: Pantheon.

Mitchinson, Wendy. 1991. *The Nature of Their Bodies: Women and Their Doctors in Victorian Canada*. Toronto: University of Toronto Press.

Morantz-Sanchez, Regina. 1985. 'The Female Student Has Arrived: The Rise of the Women's Medical Movement.' In *'Send Us a Lady Physician': Women Doctors in America, 1835–1920*, ed. Ruth J. Abram, 59–69. New York: Norton.

Neiswander, Judith. 1988. 'Liberalism, Nationalism and the Evolution of Middle-class Values: The Literature on Interior Decoration in England, 1875–1914.' PhD diss., University of London.

Ng, Roxanna. 1987. 'Immigrant Women in the Labour Force: An Overview of Present Knowledge and Research Gaps.' *Resources for Feminist Research* 16/1 (March): 29–33.

Nochlin, Linda. 1988. *Women, Art, and Power and Other Essays*. New York: Harper & Row.

Oakley, Ann. 1974. *Woman's Work: The Housewife, Past and Present*. London: A. Lane.

'Opportunities for Young Architects Are Plentiful but Best Are Found in Our Smaller, Growing Cities.' 1949. *Financial Post*, 19 April, 18.

Osborne, Milton S. 1941. 'School of Architecture, University of Manitoba.' *RAIC Journal* 18/2 (February): 20.

Parr, Joy, ed. 1995. *A Diversity of Women: Ontario, 1945–1980*. Toronto: University of Toronto Press.

Parry, B. Evan. 1935. 'Architecture to the Fore.' *RAIC Journal* 12/12 (December): 204–5.

'Place Bonaventure.' 1967. *Architecture Canada* (July): 31–9.

Pollock, Griselda. 1988. *Vision and Difference: Femininity, Feminism and the Histories of Art*. London and New York: Routledge.

Prentice, Alison, Paula Bourne, Gail Cuthbert Brandt, Beth Light, Wendy Mitchinson, and Naomi Black. 1988. *Canadian Women: A History*. Toronto: Harcourt Brace Jovanovich.

Profiles: Pioneering Women Architects from Finland. c. 1983. Helsinki: Museum of Finnish Architecture.'

Rex, Kay. 1962. 'Remodels old houses.' *Globe and Mail*, 25 October, 19.

Rinfret, Natalie. 1997. 'Le style de gestion des hommes et des femmes: convergence ou divergence?' Communication au Congrès AIEIA, juillet.

Ringon, Gérard. n.d. 'Histoire du métier d'architecte.' Enseignement 1310, Université de Toulouse–Le Mirail.

Robson, Philip A. 1929. *Architecture as a Career: A Manual for Aspirants and Students of Either Sex.* London: Batsford.

Rosin, Hazel M., and Karen Korabik. 1991a. 'Executive Women: A Close-Up View of the Corporate Experience.' *Equal Opportunities International* 10, 3/4: 38–45.

– 1991b. 'Workplace Variables, Affective Responses, and Intention to Leave Among Women Managers.' *Journal of Occupational Psychology* 64: 317–30.

– 1992. 'Corporate Flight of Women Managers: Moving from Fiction to Fact.' *Women in Management Review* 7/3: 31–5.

Rossiter, Margaret. 1978. 'Sexual Segregation in the Sciences: Some Data and a Model.' *Signs, Journal of Women in Culture and Society* 4/1: 146–51.

Ruskin, John. n.d. *Sesames and Lilies.* Chicago: Donahue.

Russell, John A. 1954. 'Architectural Education at the University of Manitoba, 1913–1953.' *RAIC Journal* 31/3 (March): 63.

Ryan, Mary. 1990. *Women in Public: Between Banners and Ballots, 1825–1880.* Baltimore: Johns Hopkins University Press.

Saint, Andrew. 1983. *The Image of the Architect.* New Haven, CT: Yale University Press.

Sarfatti Larson, Magali. 1993. *Behind the Postmodern Facade: Architectural Change in Late Twentieth Century America.* Berkeley: University of California Press.

Savage, Mike. 1992. 'Women's Expertise, Men's Authority: Gendered Organisations and the Contemporary Middle Classes.' In *Gender and Bureaucracy*, ed. Mike Savage and Anne Witz, 124–51. Oxford: Blackwell.

Schirmer, Gretchen, and Peta Tancred. 1996. 'Women's Participation within Male Parameters: The Official Presence of Women in Engineering Associations.' Paper delivered at CSAA Annual Meeting. Brock University, St Catharines, June.

Schmertz, Mildred, ed. 1987. *Contemporary Architects.* New York: St Martin's Press.

Scully, Vincent. 1971. *The Shingle Style and the Stick Style.* New Haven, CT: Yale University Press.

Shaw, Janet. 1956. 'A New Yardstick for School Building Costs.' *Canadian Builder* (October): 31–40.

'She Believes Architecture Is a "Natural" for Women.' 1944. *Montreal Daily Star*, 21 June, 12.

Simmins, Geoffrey. 1982/3. 'Joan Burt: Feisty Toronto Architect Has to Carve Her Own Niche.' *City & Country Home* (Winter): 148.

– 1989. *Ontario Association of Architects: A Centennial History, 1889–1989.* Toronto: OAA.

Smyth, Elizabeth, Sandra Acker, Paula Bourne, and Alison Prentice, eds. 1999.

Challenging Professions: Historical and Contemporary Perspectives on Women's Professional Work. Toronto: University of Toronto Press.

Sokoloff, Natalie J. 1992. *Black Women and White Women in the Professions.* New York: Routledge.

Spain, Daphne. 1992. *Gendered Spaces.* Chapel Hill: University of North Carolina Press.

Stanton, Danielle. 1997. 'Lâcheuses, les femmes? Non: Innovatrices.' *La Gazette des femmes* (January/February): 11–12.

Statistics Canada. 1995. *Women in Canada: A Statistical Report.* Ottawa: Industry Canada.

– 1997. *1996 Census Handbook.* Ottawa: Industry Canada.

Stern, Madeleine. 1959. 'America's First Woman Architect.' *Journal of the Society of Architectural Historians* 18/2 (May): 66.

Stimpson, Catharine, ed. 1981. *Women and the American City.* Chicago: University of Chicago Press.

Strong-Boag, Veronica. 1981. 'Canada's Women Doctors: Feminism Constrained.' In *Medicine in Canadian Society: Historical Perspectives*, ed. S.E.D. Shortt, 207–35. Montreal and Kingston: McGill-Queen's University Press.

Symons, Gladys L. 1984. 'Career Lives of Women in France and Canada: The Case of Managerial Women.' *Work and Occupations* 11 (August): 331–52.

Tancred, Peta. 1995. 'Women's Work: A Challenge to the Sociology of Work.' *Gender, Work and Organization* 2/1: 11–20.

Tancred, Peta, Marianne Ainley, Gillian Rejskind, and Susan Whitesides. 1994. 'Critical Turning Points: Women Engineers Within and Outside the Profession.' Description of Proposed Research, Part A. Ottawa: Social Sciences and Humanities Research Council.

Tancred, Peta, and Susan Czarnocki. 1993. '"The Revolving Door": Women's Exit from Non-Traditional Work.' In *Weaving Alliances*, ed. Debra Martens, 97–120. Ottawa: Canadian Women's Studies Association.

– 1998. 'The Revolving Door: Faculty Women Who Exit Academia.' In *The Illusion of Inclusion*, ed. Jacqueline Stalker and Susan Prentice, 119–32. Halifax: Fernwood.

Tancred-Sheriff, Peta. 1989. 'Gender, Sexuality and the Labour Process.' In *The Sexuality of Organization*, ed. Jeff Hearn, Deborah L. Sheppard, Peta Tancred-Sheriff, and Gibson Burrell, 45–55. London: Sage.

Torre, Susana, ed. 1977. *Women in American Architecture: A Historic and Contemporary Perspective.* New York: Whitney.

Townsend, C.H. 1886. 'Women as Architects.' *British Architect* (31 December): vii–viii.

Tremblay, Katia. 1993a. 'Accession des femmes à l'enseignement supérieur et origines d'une practique architecturale féminine.' In ACFAS, *Les Bâtisseuses de la Cité*, 173–91. Montreal: Université de Montréal, Congrès de l'Acfas.

- 1993b. 'Les origines d'une pratique architecturale féminine au Québec: Henriette Barrot Chenevert et Pauline Roy Rouillard, deux pionnières.' M. Arch., Université Laval.

van Ginkel, Blanche Lemco. 1991. 'Slowly and Surely (and Somewhat Painfully): More or Less the History of Women in Architecture in Canada.' *Bulletin of the Society for the Study of Architecture in Canada* 17/1 (March): 6–11.

- 1993. *Canadian Architect* (November): 15–17.

Van Slyck, Abigail A. 1992. 'Women in Architecture and the Problems of Biography.' *Design Book Review* 25 (Summer): 19–22.

Viloria, James A. 1994. 'Place Bonaventure: Process, Form, and Interpretation.' MA in Art History thesis, Concordia University.

Vipond, Mary. 1977. 'The Image of Women in Mass Circulation Magazines in the 1920s.' In *The Neglected Majority: Essays in Canadian Women's History*, ed. Alison Prentice and Susan Mann Trofimenkoff, 116–24. Toronto: McClelland & Stewart.

Waite, Linda J., and Sue E. Berryman. 1985. *Women in Non-Traditional Occupations: Choice and Turnover.* Santa Monica, CA: Rand.

Walker, Lynne. 1984. *Women Architects: Their Work.* London: Sorella.

- 1989. 'Women in Architecture.' In *A View from the Interior*, ed. Judy Attfield and Pat Kirkham, 90–105. London: Women's Press.

Weisman, Leslie Kanes. 1992. *Discrimination by Design: A Feminist Critique of the Man-Made Environment.* Urbana: University of Illinois Press.

Wekerle, Gerda. 1980. 'Women in the Urban Environment.' *Signs, Journal of Women in Culture and Society* 5/3 (Suppl.) (Spring): S188–214.

- 1991. *Canadian Women's Housing Projects.* Ottawa: Canada Mortgage and Housing Corporation.

Wekerle, Gerda, Rebecca Peterson, and David Morley, eds. 1980. *New Space for Women.* Boulder, CO: Westview.

'"We Knew What We Wanted."' 1949. *Canadian Homes and Gardens* 26/12 (December): 32–3, 66.

Willis, Julie. 1997. 'Women in Architecture in Victoria, 1905–1955: Their Education and Professional Life.' PhD diss., University of Melbourne.

Witz, Anne. 1990. 'Patriarchy and Professions: The Gendered Politics of Occupational Closure.' *Sociology* 24/4: 675–90.

- 1992. *Professions and Patriarchy.* London: Routledge.

'Women as Architects.' 1911. *Saturday Night* 24 (22 April): 8.

'Women Never Invent Anything.' 1876. *Englishwoman's Review* 7 (15 March): 108–13.

Wright, Gwendolyn. 1977. 'On the Fringe of the Profession: Women in American Architecture.' In *The Architect: Chapters in the History of the Profession*, ed. Spiro Kostof, 280–308. Oxford: Oxford University Press.

Index

Mactavish, Janet Leys Shaw, 75, 76 (fig. 4.10), 77 (fig. 4.11)

Manicouagan 5 dam, 117

Manitoba, 15, 16; *see also* Manitoba Association of Architects, University of Manitoba

Manitoba Association of Architects: entry to, 17 (table 2.1), 136 (table B.7); founding of, 15, 7n. 153; members leaving, 27 (table 2.4); women members of, 23 (tables 2.3A and 2.3B), 137 (table B.8), 138 (table B.9)

Manotick, 83 (fig. 4.13), 84

Marani, Lawson and Morris, 41

marine architecture, 149, 153n. 6

marital status, 145 (table B.16); of architects, 22, 56, 67, 70, 88; and images, 47, 49 (fig. 3.5); in interviews, 90–1; and professional advancement, 54–5; and women's rights, 114

Marshall & Merrett, 72, 74, 75

masculinity, 11, 37, 51–7, 67

Massachusetts Institute of Technology, 70

'material feminists,' 4

Mathers and Haldenby, 41

McGill University: buildings at, 72, 73 (fig. 4.8); entry of women to, 18 (table 2.2), 40, 78, 157n. 16; ghetto, 64; graduates of, 9, 59, 75, 80 (fig. 4.12), 84, 113; program at, 165n. 10

McKay, Sherry, 78–9

McNab, Duncan, 78

McRoberts, Kenneth, 117

medical profession, 6, 7, 37–8, 90, 115–16, 122, 133 (table B.4), 162n. 26, 168n. 12

men: in advertisements, 47, 48 (fig. 3.4), 49 (fig. 3.5), 50; alternative employment, 32–5; architects, 43, 51–4, 56, 57, 62, 64, 67, 70–1, 86–7, 139 (table B.10); in census, 21–2; and de-registration, 89–90, 92–4; domination of the profession, 9–10, 11, 13, 106–10, 122–3; and education, 140 (table B.11); and employment, 141 (table B.12), 142 (table B.13); and ethnicity, 143 (table B.14); and immigration, 146 (tables B.17 and B.18); in interviews, 128–9; and language, 144 (table B.15); and marital status, 145 (table B.16); and registration, 24–6; and space, 38; *see also* husbands, masculinity

Miller, J. Abbot, 45

Mitchell, Juliet, 113, 118

mobility, 93, 27 (table 2.4), 113, 147 (table B.19), 148 (table B.20), 149, 167n. 4

Modernism: in British Columbia, 153n. 10; definition of, 152n. 12; of Le Corbusier, 56; masculinity and, 11; women architects' role in, 37, 62–3, 67, 72, 75–6, 78, 81, 82, 117–18

Montreal: buildings in, 70; opportunities for women architects in, 54, 60–2, 63–5, 67, 68 (fig. 4.4), 69 (figs. 4.5 and 4.6), 72, 73 (fig. 4.8), 74, 75, 76 (fig. 4.10), 81, 87, 117, 118; photographs of, 128; and religion, 116; *see also* École des Beaux Arts, McGill University

Morgan, Julia, 10

motherhood. *See* children

mothers of architects. *See* parents

museum, 32

naval architecture, 84, 149, 153n. 6, 161n. 56

Nelson, 70

DATE DUE
DATE DE RETOUR

ARR McLEAN   38-296

'DESIGNING WOMEN'

Gender and the Architectural Profession

Historically, the contributions of women architects to their profession have been minimized or overlooked. *'Designing Women'* explores the tension that has existed between the architectural profession and its women members. It demonstrates the influence that these women have had on architecture in Canada, and links their so-called marginalization to the profession's restrictive and sometimes discriminatory practices.

Co-written by an architectural historian and a sociologist, this book provides a welcome blend of disciplinary approaches. The product of much original research, it looks at issues that are specific to architecture in Canada and at the same time characteristic of many male-dominated workplaces.

Annmarie Adams and Peta Tancred examine the issue of gender and its relation to the larger dynamics of status and power. They argue that many women architects have reacted with ingenuity to the difficulties they have faced, making major innovations in practice and design. Branching out into a wide range of alternative fields, these women have extended and developed what are considered to be the core specializations within architecture. As the authors point out, while the profession 'designs' women's place within it, women design buildings and careers that transcend that narrow professional definition.

ANNMARIE ADAMS is an associate professor of architecture at McGill University.
PETA TANCRED is a professor of sociology at McGill University.